No Stone Unturned:

*How My Special Needs Child
and I Transformed Against All Odds*

A Memoir

DEBRA TAUBENSLAG

As a thank you for purchasing *No Stone Unturned,* please visit my website at
https://www.debrataubenslag.com/freebies
and enter your email address to receive your free gifts: a self-awareness quiz that will enlighten you and a deeply relaxing meditation.

Thanks again,
Deb

Library of Congress Control Number: 2020922754
Publishing Coordinator – Sharon Kizziah-Holmes

Published by Dove Keeper Press – USA

ISBN -13: 978-0-578-76068-1

Dedication

To my parents,
Elliott and Myrna Taubenslag

I believe we choose our parents before we are born, and everyone has to agree. Thank you for consenting to be the ones who would teach me about giving generously of heart and mind, never giving up, and the importance of being humble while you serve. You supported me in all my adventures, spiritual views of life, and most of all helping to raise Nick. I could not have done it myself because it truly does take a village—and you were there from the beginning to the end of your lives.

I began writing this book before you moved back up North from Florida. For four years the book sat undisturbed, patiently waiting to be finished when the time was right. After you both passed, I felt you nudge me from spirit to start writing again. I felt driven. The most amazing thing: the words just flowed through me like your endless love. I still get goosebumps. I love you forever.

CONTENTS

FORWARD

Once in a while, you read a book that speaks to you where you really live and makes you a better person. *No Stone Unturned: How My Special Needs Child and I Transformed Against All Odds* does just that and so much more: it brings out the best in YOU.

Simple to read yet profoundly wise, Debra Taubenslag, and her son, Nicholas, share intimate details of how to navigate challenges, possibilities and emerge with clarity so that you, and those around you, "Imagine and create the best possible outcome in every situation."

So if you are ready to take it a little easier and make a monumental difference in your life and the life of an extra-ordinary special needs person this book is a must read for YOU.

It's a real page-turner! As an amazing bonus, each chapter ends with practical ideas that you can immediately apply to your life. I for one am so much better for having read this powerful book and you will be too.

Shelley Stockwell-Nicholas, PhD
President of the International Hypnosis Federation

INTRODUCTION

When I was a young girl, I realized I was different from my peers. I was quiet and reserved; yet I was very sensitive to other people's feelings. I had a select few friends who would come into my life quickly and then leave when circumstances separated us. Like me, these friends were usually people who did not fit in well. Whether through divorce, adoption, foster childhood or race, they were all different in some way. I could *feel* their loneliness or low self-esteem. Naturally, I gravitated toward them because I understood. I was what we would now call an "empath" but did not know this at the time.

As I became a teenager, all of my classmates were busy figuring out what they wanted to major in at college. I knew I was going to attend college, but I really didn't care what my major or possible career would be. All I ever really wanted in life was to be a mom. Family was comforting for me and represented security. To nurture and be compassionate came naturally to me. That's all I really knew about myself.

How devastating it was for me then, to be told at age 23 that I could never have children due to excess scar tissue caused by endometriosis. I cried and cried for my lost dreams and grieved internally for years. Then at the age of 27, I was shocked to find out that I had become pregnant.

I was single with a mediocre, low-paying dead-end job. I didn't know how I was going to do it but felt thrilled to see my life-long dream coming true. Of course, I was scared, but I had a deep conviction in my heart that this child was "a gift from God." My silent prayer had been heard and answered!

Imagine how I felt when I gave birth to a peanut at 29 weeks. The neonatologist and staff were trying to prepare me to accept the likelihood of his death and/or severe disability. But I knew deep down inside that my son would survive, that he had been given to me for a reason. Of course, I had no idea at the time what that higher purpose might be besides for me to love him.

I remember making a pact with God then. I had no religious beliefs, but, when you are desperate, you begin to acknowledge a power greater than yourself. I told God that if He saved my son I would do whatever He wanted. I would serve Him and do His bidding. I had no clue what form that service might take, but I believed God would guide me or show me what to do along the way. I believed that as long as I remained open to all possibilities, the path would present itself to me.

Decades have passed and writing this memoir of raising my son Nick has helped me realize what my service has been: To discover, clarify, and guide the personal transformations and spiritual awakenings of others. Everyone has gifts and every soul, a purpose. I see it as my calling to help others find their purpose.

Sounds lofty and a bit heady, I know. But it's true. Helping Nick discover who he is and why he is here has assisted him in seeing the bigger picture: his *life purpose*. In doing so, he has helped many others. And so have I. It started a domino effect which in turn has led to a "butterfly effect" that can transform anyone who chooses to travel this path to awakening.

It has been a continual journey of self-discovery for both of us. We have employed countless techniques from various cultures, centuries, and belief systems. The plan of action was to *leave no stone unturned.*

Nick has healed on many levels and to varying degrees. Many say it was a miracle. I believe he has tapped into his own inner beliefs and thought processes by moving beyond "normal" consciousness.

By helping Nick, I healed as well. To this day, my son has been and continues to be my greatest teacher. You might be saying, "Oh my child is too severely disabled," or "My child's behavior is too violent," or "My child is too medically compromised." You may find yourself thinking, "I am too burnt out to try something new," or "I am too angry, too frustrated, too resentful, too lonely, and too sad."

I understand completely, because my son and I have endured all of these rollercoaster emotions as well.

I didn't dwell too long in the dark pit, however, for I knew that this would neither serve me nor my son. Whenever I felt those emotions building inside me, I would retreat to the privacy of my room or to the car to be alone. I would ask God, Spirit, or a departed loved one to help me release the heavy load that I was carrying. A wave of emotion would swirl within me like a cyclone until it rose to my throat and screamed out a sob. Explosive sobbing would follow.

Funny how I would feel like I split into two bodies: the sufferer who was releasing the emotional burden and the quiet observer compassionately waiting for the "steam to escape from the pressure cooker." This detached self-observation worked for me. Within a few minutes I would always regain my composure and carry on.

My intention in writing this book is to invite you to explore another way of coping, a different way of interpreting your experiences. I would like to open your mind to non-conventional options, including spiritual and metaphysical healing modalities. Opening and elevating your consciousness will ultimately result in personal transformation both for you and for all who follow you. You will gain new insights into the lessons of your own life and of your child's as well. More importantly, you will discover your life purpose, which is inseparable from your experience with your special needs child.

Healing comes in all forms. There is no right way or wrong way to heal. I would like to show you an alternative way of viewing your child's struggles by which both of you may benefit, grow, and expand your possibilities.

I am not saying this journey is a *cure*. I am saying that when you discover your innate gifts and when you consciously choose to change your inner thoughts, that is when a shift occurs and magic happens. Miracles transpire large and small, and each one of us is worthy and entitled to love, a sense of purpose and the experience of joy in its fullest expression.

I hope that after reading our story, you will explore and try some of the techniques and strategies that have worked for us. Perhaps you will also gain answers to the following questions that might stir in your mind:

- How do I release frustration, anger, and grief in order to feel alive and experience a sense of freedom?
- How do I heal the relationships that matter most?
- How do I recapture joy?
- Why me?
- What is my life purpose?

Everyone is entitled to and worthy of "creating" their own transformation. This is a memoir of how my son Nick and I did it. Take what you can. If it makes sense to you, then try it.

If not, let it go and move on. Some of what you are about to read will hopefully ring true for you. All I ask is that you "pay it forward" by sharing what you learn with others.

CHAPTER 1

TRANSFORMATION:

What I Learned About Belief, the Power of My Thoughts and How it Directly Affected My Child

Thirty-four magical years have flown by. Sometimes they were very long years. Some were easy but never normal. What is normal anyway? Don't we all have quirks and things we keep hidden from others? I decided it was time to tell you about my quirky and not so normal life. A life filled with love, learning, and magical moments.

It all began when my son Nicholas was born. My transformation perhaps began even earlier since I had anything but a normal pregnancy.

Nick was born at 29 weeks. I never felt him kick or let me know he was in there. I just grew big even though I gave birth to a very tiny preemie.

I used to say, "I thought he was gas." I didn't know I was in labor pain. Years later I joked with him that he came out like diarrhea, for I couldn't stop him from wanting to come out as early as he did. I learned that this was part of his divine plan, written in his astrological natal chart, and decided by him before he was born. But I will tell you about this later.

The nurses and doctors in the NIC (no pun intended) tried to tell me that if he survived he would have several severe complications due to a brain bleed, including hydrocephalus that developed a few days after birth. They thought I was in denial.

I believed differently. My mind trusted in the psychic I saw (while I was pregnant and not showing). She told me I was carrying a male child and that, no matter what the doctors said, I should feel confident in the fact that he would survive and thrive.

Everyone else worried while I sang show tunes and lullabies. I went to the hospital every day for three months because I felt it was important for him to "sense" I was with him. So he wouldn't feel abandoned when I went home for the night, I left a tape recorder with my voice talking to him while he slept in his isolette.

All kinds of tubes ran up and down his body. I wanted to hold him, but I obviously couldn't. Instead, I would massage the outline of his body so gently and slowly while imagining that he felt my tender touch. As I did this, the monitor would show that his heart rate and breathing slowed to a comfortable relaxed, rhythmic pace.

How healing this was for me when I felt so helpless. This simple act with my imagination, intention, and passing movements with my hands made a difference for both of us. I felt I was helping. I knew I was. What a gift to know that I could actually do something to make him feel better. This comforted me greatly and, of course, did the same for him.

Finally, after three months and two brain surgeries, Nick weighed enough for me to bring him home. Now the real work needed to be done: infant stimulation, early intervention, and "tap the unused portion of his brain to compensate." What a journey—one we are still on. We discovered, explored and learned so much. Leaving no stone unturned. Yes, we experienced a lot of frustration, which I called "growing pains," and anger, sadness, and grief but also laughter, wonder, and awe. Magical moments.

Those were the best. Magical moments that took my breath away and inwardly made me smile at the magnificence of small and large miracles.

What I learned:

- To trust in what *you* know to be true. It doesn't matter what others say and think. What matters is to *know what you know*.

- To believe that *what you think* counts because it *does*. *You* matter.

- Our thoughts are energy. They have form and are real. Energy has power and positive energy can be life changing. So can negative energy. If you think it's bad, then it is. If you think it's okay, then it is. It is what it is.

- To *believe* in miracles.

Nick at one month old after his first brain surgery.

CHAPTER 2

STIMULATION:

What I Learned About the Potential of the Mind and Not Getting Lost in the Process

Infant stimulation and early intervention; that's what the experts said would help with developmental delays. Since I quit my job the day my son was born so prematurely, I began a new occupation, learning about how to stimulate the brain and help it to talk to his body parts. I read everything I could, spoke to all kinds of therapists, and became a mother on a mission who believed that anything was possible.

Nick went to a specialized institute three times a week for two hours each session. There I learned how to work with his brain by playing with toys and exercising his limbs. Nick's legs were always changing—sometimes rigid as a rod, sometimes spastic or floppy like a rag doll. He didn't speak, and it looked like his eyes were empty. I remember thinking, "his soul is not in his body." It was an odd, depressing thought but it felt true.

Many years later a well-known and respected healer told me that my son's soul did not enter his body until he was sure he was "staying." I found that statement to be powerfully accurate because I witnessed it. I remember feeling great relief when I finally saw a spark in his eye. I knew then that he had finally arrived.

I kept up the exercises and play at home every day. My Dad would write and tell animated stories while my brother Michael would act out the characters. Even my Mom got involved when we all sang and danced to *Singing in the Rain* with umbrellas. Nick was continuously stimulated in my house. We were all working together as one team. We were all on a mission to help Nick learn, grow, laugh, and be as *normal* as possible.

I was determined to make him catch up no matter what the cost. And there was a cost. For some reason in the early years of this journey, I believed that, if I was even briefly distracted from Nick and my mission, I would lose momentum and shatter, literally break, and Nick would lose precious irreversible development time. I thought of Anne Sullivan, the great give-it-all-you've-got teacher who taught Hellen Keller.

Nothing stopped her and nothing would stop me.

I actually believed that if I received a healing touch from anyone I would not be able to heal my son. How ironic that Nick benefited greatly from my healing touch, and yet I couldn't receive it back. I remained physically and emotionally untouched for two years. What a foolish thought that created a senseless belief, which created a ludicrous outcome for me.

What I learned:

- "Stupid is stupid," as Forest Gump would say.

- The brain is a powerful organ, but the mind is greater and much more powerful.

- Stimulation and exercise are vital at any age.

- Thoughts and beliefs create outcomes, and they can harm or heal.

- Family is love and comes in many forms: actual family, friends, therapists, and kind strangers. Asking for support helps them show love.

My brother, Michael, doing infant stimulation
by reading to Nick

Nick as a happy toddler at age two.

Nick, my dad, Elliott, my brother, Michael, and I
posing for a photo shoot for the family
children's theater business.

The story comes to life when "Tex" comes to visit.

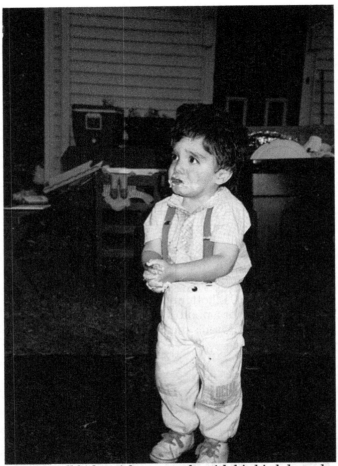

Just like all kids, Nick got caught with his birthday cake
on his face. Adorable.

CHAPTER 3

PERCEPTION:

What I Learned About Viewing My World: Half Empty or Half Full

"Little children, little problems; big children, big problems" was a phrase my Great Grandma Bubba used to say. The preschool years were heaven. Yes, he was developmentally delayed in almost everything. It didn't matter what he couldn't do. I figured he would get there eventually. I focused on what he could do and celebrated each milestone with praise and honest joy.

My twin brother had a child soon after me. He was seemingly perfect in every way. Unlike me, my sister-in-law recorded every milestone and kept mental, dated notes of everything my son achieved too. This ultimately helped me cope and stay focused on *achieving* with Nick while avoiding resentment. I would hear all about my nephew's accomplishments and genuinely be happy for her. I chose not to dwell or think about Nick's delays, so she became a great resource for me whenever I needed to recall dates and fill out official forms.

By age three, Nick was enrolled in a handicap preschool program. He thrived there. The early intervention continued and we watched him bloom.

At the same time, I met a wonderful man who became a dear friend. With time, we fell in love and eventually married. He decided to take on the role of teacher to my son. He used to say, "He doesn't have to like me as long as he learns."

I didn't agree with his philosophy. He was tough, firm and taught Nick how to hop, jump, and climb stairs. He tried to teach him how to ride a bike, but unfortunately I stopped him because my son was screaming bloody murder every time they attempted it. I was too soft and wrong. I should have allowed the *tough love* because he still doesn't ride a bike or drive. Both my dad and husband believed he could have done it. I was too protective and regret it now.

In elementary school, Nick was always in the corner in time out. When I called a meeting with the kindergarten teacher and guidance counselor, I was informed that he was "kicked out" of her classroom. It was then they told me he had to join a small special-ed class. After my ego healed, I realized that it was a blessing in disguise. He received every support available: PT, OT, speech therapy, and individualized attention. He became a wonderful student.

Only one bad thing occurred: A school psychologist insisted that the only way back into the classroom was to be put on Ritalin. I didn't like it but I agreed. I felt I didn't have a choice at the time. It was 1990 and there were no other options. Everything happens for a reason though. It spurred me to research every holistic and metaphysical avenue out there, a continual driven journey I am still on.

What I learned:

- Every situation has a positive and negative, and perception is key. How you view it matters most.

- As my psychic friend Jack told me, it's not my job to calm a storm. It's my job to calm myself because storms always pass.

- Everything happens for a reason even though you can't see it at the time.

- There is a huge world out there with information and answers. You just have to reach out and ask.

CHAPTER 4

THERAPIES AND REMEDIES:

What I Learned About Conventional, Unconventional, and Otherworldly Trials

During the primary years, we kept busy exploring therapies and remedies. So many—where do I begin? I'll start with remedies first because I felt they were the easiest, and I could do work on them at home.

Better nutrition was first on the list. Every parent knows how tricky it is to get your child to eat vegetables and eliminate junk food and sugar. I decided early on to never, ever buy soda. The only sweets in our home were baked by my husband, and, of course, we had fruit. Even the jelly and peanut butter had no added sugar. Did it help? I don't know but I felt I had some control over his diet, which, in essence, eased my mind.

I installed full spectrum light bulbs so Nick could receive the benefit of having as much "natural" light as possible. I also investigated nutritional supplementation and found that DHEA was the latest and greatest in the late '80s and '90s, so it was added to his morning Ritalin regimen.

Lavender baths helped him to relax and calm down. This was a godsend. He still takes aromatherapy baths combined with Epsom salts at age 34. That's how terrific this simple remedy is.

Regarding therapy, he underwent multiple kinds; including traditional, metaphysical and other experiential ways to accept and love himself and move forward. Remediation was experienced in school: physical, occupational and speech therapy during pullout time from special ed. His self-esteem was actually pretty high at the time because he didn't know that he was "different." He assumed that everyone thought and behaved like he did. Nick even ran for Sergeant at Arms in elementary school twice in two years, believing he could win. The principal told me that he received only one vote, his own, but she loved his enthusiasm and resilience. The behavioral and emotional problems didn't begin until middle school. That was when he realized he was, in fact, considerably different, and he didn't like himself because of it. He would say that he had good self-esteem, but parents always know, right?

At this point all kinds of emotional therapy began. He received traditional psychotherapy for decades. Nick always lied to his therapist and never did his therapy homework. Looking back now, it may have been somewhat of a waste of time and money and a source of frustration for all of us.

We kept it up though for decades because desperation encourages you to keep going. The only positive that came about was that we discovered that Nick *loved* psychodrama and role-playing. When I think back, this is no surprise since he is a kinesthetic learner as well as an empath, so, of course, he would connect to this type of therapy.

I also continued to give him massages and hands-on healing along with clinical and spiritual hypnosis. (Right after Nick's birth, I received massage training and certification, a doctorate in Clinical Hypnosis, and a Special Education Teaching degree.) Massage allowed him to relax and feel comfortable in his body. Hands-on healing helped him to "feel" energy and changed his mood. Hypnosis, especially spiritual hypnosis, gave him an opportunity to "feel" his feelings and recognize his innate gifts and divine purpose.

I knew this was important because when he was three he told me had a dream but had trouble expressing it. I told him to draw it, but that ended up looking like a colorful scribble.

Then he looked up and said, "Everybody's God." He was three. What three-year-old has a concept of God or an understanding that we are all connected and one with God? It made me realize that the veil between our consciousness and otherworld realities is thin during our early years. That is why I never told him it was his imagination when a being named Barbara tapped him on the shoulder periodically to remind him to pay attention. Nor did I discount his friend Timmy on the little bus who the bus driver said was nonexistent. I have learned that just because we can't see, hear, or feel something doesn't mean it doesn't exist. Nick's experiences were real and comforting to him. I am glad he experienced this. It fostered a lifetime of love and learning for spirituality, humanism, activism, and healing.

Spiritual hypnosis was just one of many modalities he experienced. Some of the others that are considered nonconventional are:

- Vision therapy (It's not what you think; it trains the brain.)
- Anger workshops (to get in touch with his emotions)
- Yoga (to help him relax and stretch his tight muscles)
- Taekwondo (for focus, concentration, fitness and self-esteem)
- Acupuncture (for correct energy flow and balance)
- Meditation (for peace, calming, and insight)

- Natal and vocational astrological charts (to understand himself better and learn about possible career options to consider)
- Music/sound therapy (i.e., Mozart for focus, Bach for relaxation, and instrumental CDs to help uplift)
- Drama club and summer theatre (to feel included)
- Choir (for joy)
- Reiki (to feel energy and to be of service)
- Inspirational films (for teachable lessons)
- Flower remedies and essential oils (to stabilize emotions)
- Vision boards (to manifest clear dreams into reality)
- Mankind Project (to learn and feel connection to others and self-acceptance)
- Angel and oracle cards (for introspection)
- Image dressing (for confidence and personal style; *Queer Eye for the Straight Guy* was beneficial.)
- Intuitive guidance from psychic healers (for confirmation and to be *heard* and understood)
- Drum circles (for connection)
- Writing (for creative expression)
- Breathwork (for releasing old emotions and wounds)
- Cognitive therapy & metronome (to retrain and balance hemispheric communication)

- Alpha-Stim or CES Ultra (to relieve anxiety and depression using an at-home cranial electrotherapy device approved by the FDA)

What I learned:

- Some things work, some do not, and some work better than others.

- If there is a glimmer of hope, keep it up. Anything worthwhile takes time.

- Pick your battles. "Some things are worth falling on your sword for."

- Keep searching till you find something that clicks. Self-esteem, connection to others, and sense of purpose is what matters most.

CHAPTER 5

CONNECTION:
What I Learned About the Need to Be Loved, Included, and Needed

Friends accept and love us and bring us joy. We wear no masks and thrive in the presence of their company. We know our backs are covered and our love is reciprocated. Because the connection we feel is more than comfortable, no special effort is required. Friendship is our safe haven. We can truly be loved and accepted for our uniqueness, forgiven for our mishaps, and applauded for our accomplishments.

Unfortunately, my son struggled with this basic human right. It pained me to see that he was not invited to birthday parties nor asked to play with anyone. He lacked social skills, and setting boundaries was a huge lesson he never really learned. We used to practice two steps forward, one step back (literally) so he would not be in someone's physical space. This was exceedingly hard for him because of his problem with visual/spacial perception. His constant interruptions, impulsivity, and lack of understanding of social etiquette were equally difficult.

He also had issues with executive functioning, an aspect of brain function that controls so much of what we need to survive and thrive in the world. Imagine walking on Broadway in New York City, unable to filter out the sights, sounds, and congestion of people walking. They are bumping into you as you try to navigate and move forward to your intended direction. Imagine how this would feel knowing you are alone, without friends, and the only ones who care about you are your parents who seem to always "nag." It's an existence that is utterly lonely and depressing.

I had tried everything to teach him ways to make and keep a friend. His behavior always got in the way. I realized no amount of pleading, crying, and coercing would alter the behavior. I couldn't do it. He had to be the one to change, and I couldn't transform him no matter how badly I wanted to.

He shunned the idea of reaching out to other special needs kids for decades. Perhaps in some way befriending others like him forced him to accept his disability and in turn himself. It was like looking into a mirror and hating what you saw. He was not ready to face who he was and tried to be accepted by people who did not want to befriend him.

Rejection was the common theme that played over and over in both friendships and love interests. He didn't see how he was discouraging those who would love him and alienating those who wouldn't. It wasn't until his early thirties that he finally came to terms with who he was and learn to not only accept himself but to embrace his "specialness" and life purpose.

Now, finally, he has made a few acquaintances by joining a Friday night adult club and a Saturday social program for people with disabilities and attending a Unitarian church and a NAMI Young Adult Social Club on Sundays. He works, has a massage therapy degree, Reiki 3 certification, and training as a physical therapy aide.

He discovered his life purpose through advocating. NJ Partnerships in Policymaking selected him to learn how to advocate for people with disabilities on a national, state, and local level. This training gave him the chance to express and initiate his ideas and to work on a very meaningful project that would help all special needs people in New Jersey. As is true for all of us, having a purpose is tremendously empowering and vital to Nick's self-esteem, but he needed to find it for himself.

What I learned:

- Our children need to be guided to find their own voice and their own sense of independence and achievement in order to feel authentically good about themselves.

- As parents we need to continually ask whether our expectations are too high or too low. This helps us both take a step back and look at what is going on and what really matters.

- Encourage participation in social activities no matter how discouraged or resistant. Eventually the wall will come down and a smile will crack.

- Once connections are made, invite the parents to dinner with their kid. When parents get together, it feels good for everyone and helps break initial social barriers in a relaxed, unthreatening environment. Play "Can You Top This." Note: I played this once with a mom from a regular educational program. I was telling her how my son went to sleep away camp for two months and came home with no shoes. She looked me straight in the eye and said, "Well, my son went to sleep away camp for two months and came home with unopened bags of underwear." I laughed heartily and told her she won the "Can You Top This?" game.

- Encourage being of service to someone. Edgar Cayce once said, "The only way to heaven is on the arm of someone you helped." A true friend is helpful, kind, and listens without judgment.

I kept on impressing that in order to have a friend you have to be a friend.

- Volunteerism was strongly encouraged and acted upon, which helped. So did Boy Scouts. He eventually became an Eagle Scout. Again, find something that instills self-esteem and service—whatever it takes.

CHAPTER 6

OUTCOMES:
What I Learned from Crisis

Every parent knows that gut-wrenching feeling, that fear that grips your heart when your child is in crisis and there is nothing you can do about it. The first "episode" took place when Nicholas called me one evening to say that he wasn't feeling right. I could hear that his voice was quivering, and he wasn't making any sense. He kept on repeating the same sentences over and over. Since we never experienced this before, my husband and I drove to his apartment to see if we could calm him. He had locked himself in his apartment, and we were initially only able to talk to him through his open window.

He was having a severe panic attack combined with hallucinations and delusions. We eventually got into his apartment, but my son became "the hulk" with super human strength. It took an incredible struggle on my husband's part to get him out the door and into the car to take him to the hospital.

Once there, they took blood, sedated him with Ativan, and then released him the next day with a prescription to attend an outpatient psych program. No explanation was given as to the cause of the episode. Not even a diagnosis. They needed a bed, and stabilization was their priority. They believed they did their job.

After four weeks of daily attending the outpatient program, the doctor in charge said, "He doesn't fit into our program because he is not an addict nor considered at risk."

They labeled him bipolar although he never showed signs, symptoms, or received that diagnosis before. Seven more times over a period of nine years, the experience recurred with more intense frightening hospitalizations, some life threatening because of severely depleted sodium levels. Each time another drug was added: anti-depressants, anti-anxiety, antipsychotic, and stimulants.

Again, no one was able to explain why these episodes occurred or what triggered them. Each and every specialist, psychiatrist, endocrinologist, and nephrologist said they could not help us. I became a dog with a bone; I could not give up.

The last hospitalization was very traumatic because he was sent to the ER three times in one week. Again, stabilization was the only

priority from two different hospitals. I insisted on further testing with a neurologist
.

We discovered three things:

- His shunt was disconnected at his collar bone.

- Episodes could possibly have been triggered by frontal lobe seizures which are difficult to capture on an EEG.

- During his hospital stay, we took Nick off all psychological medications after my daughter-in-law researched and discovered hallucinations and/or psychosis were listed as possible severe side effects. I am happy to report that my son has not had any more episodes and is feeling much more clear-minded and confident with himself. He initially went on the first anti-depressant as a result of feeling so angry. Being off all drugs seems to have been the best medicine for his delicate brain after all.

When I look back now, I realize that how I coped and what I did in crisis mattered greatly. The stress was so intense and literally could have killed me. Fortunately, I was able to employ the tools I used on Nick to help me.

Before I got out of bed, I took deep diaphragmatic breaths. I knew that if I slowed my breath it would calm and relax me.

Counting from 10 down to 1 helped me to relax my mind and body even more. Then I would pray and ask for guidance, protection, or healing—whatever I needed in the moment. It only took about 20 minutes, but I believe this simple morning ritual helped me get through what I needed to do. Besides, Nick would react according to my reaction. It was important that he saw I was composed and sure so he could relax and feel calm and secure. *My energy shifted his energy.*

What I learned:

- Be a mama bear and fight for what you believe is true. Those who work for our healthcare system try their best but their budgets win out.

- Some people need meds, and others don't. Don't buy into a diagnosis or RX just because an "expert" who sees your child for a few minutes thinks it's the best course. Get a second or third opinion and be persistent— pushy if you have to—until you find a doctor you can trust.

- Rely on your gut instinct. If you feel right about a course of action, then go with it. "When in doubt, throw it out." No one knows your kid better than you. Pay attention to what you *just know*.

- We are each other's mirrors. A relaxed state of mind helps everyone. Incorporating a simple morning ritual helps the whole family think and behave more peacefully.

CHAPTER 7

MENTORS:

What I Learned About the Difference They
Make and Becoming One

Even though my son had years of all kinds of therapy, he was still rejected, dismissed, and misunderstood. Yes, many teens feel like this, but when you are labeled special needs, short in stature, and your face is filled with pimples, the struggle to fit in seems insurmountable. Being bullied was a daily occurrence as was losing outerwear, books, and homework. As Kermit the frog would say, "It's not easy being green."

Nick gravitated to teachers and janitors who would help him find his things and offer guidance and kindness. They were angels as far as I was concerned.

My Dad was one of those angels too. He ran a summer theater camp and made sure

Nick was included. He knew the power of feeling purposeful, so he gave Nick jobs besides acting in the shows. Nick was the hardest worker because he thrived on feeling important and needed. It also fostered a love for theater.

I picked up on my Dad's advice and put Nick into Boy Scouts. I wanted to make sure that he would grow into manhood feeling capable and believed the experience would help him gain self-respect as well. To make sure he would not be bullied, I volunteered and became the committee chairman offering diplomacy tactics to ten other dads. Not an easy feat but one that was needed.

Because of my position, the fathers did not give my special needs son a problem. However, the one and only friend my son had at the time was rejected and bullied by some of the dads and was denied becoming an Eagle Scout because "he did not measure up" to their expectations. Needless to say, this shocked and infuriated me, especially since that boy completed all the merit badges and tasks that were required.

I researched who the CEO of the Boy Scouts of America was and wrote a strong letter about discrimination. During this time, my son's Eagle Scout Court of Honor came up. I chose not to attend because of the hypocrisy. My dad and mom represented the family for Nick in my place. To celebrate afterwards, I gave him a party and people stood up and spoke to honor Nick's accomplishments. He also received letters of congratulations from his favorite teachers, authors, state senators, and even the president's office.

In the end, my son's friend was granted a private review and received his due ceremony and deserved title. Am I sorry I did not attend my son's ceremony? Not really. I chose to be an advocate and teach my son about what's right and what's wrong. He understood why I did what I did for his friend and I believe was proud that I took a stand. It must have sunk in because twelve years later he became and still is an advocate for people with disabilities.

Another mentor was Nick's high school case manager. This man knew my son well because he took the time to get to know all his special needs students. He also kept me in the loop, which I greatly appreciated.

During Nick's senior year, I mentioned that I was let down by the school's lack of social skills training. They had study skills and, of course, all the required courses, but the one thing that most special needs kids require is social skills. He agreed. He could not change the required curriculum but suggested that Nick attend a learning disabled post-secondary sleepaway school that could help with this desired ability. All I had to do was convince the school board to pay for it. I negotiated by building a creative arts curriculum that could be incorporated by an art teacher to at least expose the arts to the students in the self-contained classes. Since I knew how my Dad's drama camp helped my son's self-esteem, I thought all the classified kids could benefit. This is how I created a successful win/win for my kid. I negotiated creatively with the help of a wonderful mentor.

What I learned:

- Feeling needed and purposeful is important to everyone.

- Follow a mentor's role and copy what's right about them.

- Advocate for what's right even if it is inconvenient, unpopular, hard, and painful. When you do right by others, you raise awareness and people notice.

- Think outside the box for something that sounds helpful and progressive. Brainstorm with mentors and people whom you trust to create positive and possible outcomes for all concerned. There is always a way.

Nick being recognized for his Eagle Scout Project:

Scout heeds Congress' call to document vets' memories

BY JEANETTE ING
Correspondent

EAST BRUNSWICK — Patriotism has become a household word these days. Duty to our country has been made manifest in bumper stickers, pins, flags, speeches, ceremonies and in the individual acts of American citizens.

One such citizen, Nick Taubenslag, a junior at East Brunswick High School, decided to channel his patriotism into a yearlong project, which culminated Sept. 28.

In some respect, the project began in October 2000 when the U.S. Congress created the Veterans History Project. Congress, knowing our veteran population fades by 1,500 each day, realized the value of a national collection of personal histories. In an effort to document these wartime memories and also engage the American public in its own history, Congress called on the nation to help create this new national collection.

By the fall 2001, Nick was at a turning point in his Boy Scout career. After seven years, he had come upon the challenge of becoming an Eagle Scout — but he needed a project that would make him worthy of the rank.

At the time, he had been reading *Was God on Vacation*, a novel by Jack VanderGeest that chronicled the life of a man following his escape from a Netherlands concentration

in participating, the project was ready. The group gathered at the veterans home the morning of Sept. 28. The day opened with a big breakfast, and ultimately 27 stories were shared and recorded.

Among them was that of Frank Ponza, a prisoner of war in Nazi Germany from December 1944 to April 1945, who recalled passing much of the time talking about food. They would eat soup every day, but food would soon be withheld from all prisoners for a time because the Germans falsely believed one of the POWs was trying to escape.

Nick Taubenslag of East Brunswick with Sal Mule, a resident of the New Jersey Veterans Memorial Home in Edison, during the Sept. 28 interview.

"Scout heeds Congress' call to document vets' memories"

CHAPTER 8

TIME OUT:
What I Learned About My Spouse When I Pulled Away from My Child

Every parent knows the challenge and heartbreak that comes with raising a special needs child, and I was no exception. When my son became angry or felt dismissed or unworthy, I was his emotional punching bag. Intellectually I understood that I was his "safe" outlet to verbally vomit.

Emotionally it took its toll on me, especially when there was no gratitude for everything I was doing for him. I felt helpless and defeated yet soldiered on. I didn't think I had a choice.

When Nick was younger, we would shop in Target, and then I would lose him because he would run off. I would search frantically until I found him making phony phone calls on the red target phone. Funny and goofy, yes. I could handle it with a sense of humor.

Another time I found him vacuuming the carpet that normally was positioned on the basement stairs. When I asked, "Why did you take the carpet off the stairs," he said it was easier to vacuum the stairs horizontally. Again, after I took a few breaths, I was able to chuckle. Even when he decided to trim the neighbor's hedges because he thought they needed a haircut, I was able to laugh it off after the neighbor was okay. She understood he was "Dennis the Menace."

However, as Nick got older, his antics were not so funny. Every day seemed to be a battle of wills. My husband would get involved to "straighten him out," which added more fuel to the fire. They constantly battled. My husband was trying to protect me and *teach* Nick how to behave at the same time. It was truly a toxic environment to live and be happy in. All of us were miserable.

I tried to be the peacemaker many, many days. Nick made an American Indian talking stick during Scouts. I would take it from his room and announce we were having a family "powwow." Whoever held the talking stick was the only person permitted to speak. No one was allowed to interrupt or speak until they held the stick. It was a temporary fix in the moment.

Finally, I reached "the straw that broke the camel's back" and went on strike from being "Mom." I couldn't take it anymore. Of course, I loved my son, but his abusive behavior towards me and his dad was literally breaking me. I actually did not talk to him for two years. I am not proud of this, but it was the only thing I could do to cope without having a mental breakdown.

This time out became magical. Without me doing *everything*, my son and husband *bonded* like never before. My husband drove him every day to the community college and picked him up, took him to every therapy appointment, and watched *24* or other bang-bang, shoot 'em up movie that I wouldn't particularly care to view. This was a miracle because I thought they hated each other.

What I learned:

- There is no such thing as a perfect parent, so forgive yourself.

- It's okay to grieve as you push on.

- I should have gone to therapy or family therapy to deal with all the screwed-up emotions.

- It took my dad saying, "If Nick could change his life, he would," to offer me a big reality check.

- Take a timeout when you need to *before it escalates.*

- Give up controlling expectations and allow family members to be who they are without constantly intervening. That's how you see who they really are and what they are made of. This journey is not only yours, it's theirs too.

- My husband surprised me with his commitment to step up and do more parenting when I let go of *control.*

My husband, Dom, and Nick.

CHAPTER 9

DISCOVERY:
What I Learned When I Let Go of My Expectations

arly on I knew I had to release my unrealistic expectations of who and what my son would become as an adult. It wasn't easy, especially since he was my only child. I had to mourn the death of my expectations for him. As all parents do, I had so many hopes and dreams. Mine needed to be adjusted; I had to remember how grateful I was that he survived and had come as far as he had.

However, I also knew there was an innate intelligence if only I could tap in to it. I was on a mission to un-tap the unused portions of the brain to compensate. Hence all the remedies and therapies; I would leave no stone unturned until I found what worked. Ironically, I believe it was the combination of *everything* we tried that helped Nick to blossom. Once he got out of his own way, the power of his mind and his belief in himself enabled him to thrive.

I know that every human being needs to feel a sense of purpose. Discovering that purpose can be challenging because most of us have no inkling what it is nor what we want to do in life. People often assume that a special needs person is limited and incapable, which makes finding and living that purpose more difficult. Stigmas, labels, and judgments are thrust upon those with special needs without giving them a chance to see what they are truly capable of doing.

In the residential post-secondary school in upstate New York, Nick was told that he would not be placed into a community college because he was "incapable" of keeping up. When he left that setting at age 21, I enrolled him in our local community college. He had to take and pass the required English and math prep courses before he could begin taking classes for credit.

The department that helps special-ed kids with tutoring and accommodations would not accept my son because he was labeled "NI – neurologically impaired" instead of "LD – learning disabled." I advocated for him heavily, including writing letters and making phone calls to the dean of the college. "Policy is policy" is what I was told.

Nick really wanted this college experience and believed he could do it. My mom tutored him in math while my dad trained him in

English. He passed. Feeling successful, he took psychology and other classes without help and thrived. Unfortunately, biology was very difficult. He took it twice and realized that maybe attending community college was not a good idea. He became despondent when he dropped out. I had to find something and discover answers quickly.

I first turned to DVR, the Division of Vocation and Rehabilitation, and they suggested he become a dog washer. This frustrated all of us because we knew he was more intelligent and more capable than what "appeared on the outside."

I researched a number of things to learn about potential careers:

- Online career testing

- *Please Understand Me*, a book that has a great assessment

- Astrological natal charts (free online) that suggested where his innate talents and gifts were and a specific astrological vocational chart that provided insights

- Spiritual hypnosis to see different paths into the future and determine where he felt comfortable, successful, and purposeful

These activities led to massage school and then Reiki. Nick did well in massage school, partly because the owner/instructor took Nick under his wing and mentored him.

A few years later he went for specialized training in Advocacy for People with Disabilities. For the first time in a long time, Nick felt good about himself. He tried several jobs in the beginning of his career that did not work out. By his mid-20s, he found a low-pressure job where he felt supported by management and accepted by his peers. Although the pay is not terrific, he has been working there part-time for nine years.

In his spare time, Nick is involved with a number of advocacy groups and participates in a variety of programs: Disability Allies, Young Adult Social Club offered through NAMI, and an adult Friday night program for people with disabilities.

He is finally comfortable with who he is because he found purpose and inclusion. As I let go of my expectations, he was liberated to find out who he truly was.

What I learned:

- Don't buy in to what other people think your children can or cannot do. No one knows their true potential except them and maybe you.

- Let them discover on their own what brings them joy. It just may surprise you how truly capable they are.

- The more I pushed the more I was pushed back.

- Explore and present other options about vocation and volunteering.

- Sometimes we have to fail in order to move forward. As Mary Pickford said, "If you have made mistakes, even serious mistakes, you may have a fresh start any moment you choose, for this thing we call "**failure**" is not the falling down but the staying down." This is good sound advice that I gave to my son and personally used on myself on many occasions.

CHAPTER 10

ACCEPTANCE:
What I Learned About Embracing Disability

How agonizing it was for me to watch my son want desperately to connect with others and painfully be rejected day after day. He was sweet, intelligent, funny, ridiculous, innocent, and naïve. I didn't understand why he didn't have any friends. You would think he would connect to other kids in his special-ed classes.

Eventually he did—but only to one. But for the longest time he had no one. I tried hard to encourage him to initiate a conversation, but unfortunately he was only asking "regular-ed" kids to be included in their adventures. He was clever enough to know that he was different but not so smart to understand that "regular-ed" kids chose not to befriend him because of that difference.

Nick fell into the cracks. He was not in the lower functioning world and not in the *regular* world. Nick was quirky, odd and, well, Nick was Nick. I used to say that a lot because it helped me to understand and better cope when I needed to.

However, Nick couldn't say that to himself. He completely denied his disability and rejected any thought of himself being different. Therefore, he refused to make friends with other kids who were disabled because in doing so it would force him to accept himself as the same.

He was bullied *a lot*. He would not tell me how often or why, but an inner rage grew and built a wall around him that no one could penetrate. He was miserable and angry. He carried a tremendous chip on his shoulder for a long time. Being short statured didn't help his self-esteem either.

He didn't realize that this anger isolated him even further. He only knew that if he built up a fortress, no one could come in and hurt him. He would lash out first before anyone else could do it to him.

Eventually he did make one friend who was in his special-ed class and Scouts. He never acknowledged that his friend had a disability as well. All he knew was that they laughed and laughed together, and that was all that mattered.

I was grateful for this friendship because every person deserves to be accepted, loved, and connected. My husband and I became friendly with the parents at the time. It helped all concerned.

One magical day, a miracle happened. I don't remember why I asked him to sit in my hypnosis chair but am joyful that I did. Within minutes he was relaxed to the point where he went into a deep hypnotic trance. I told him to "go where he needed to go, wherever that might be for his highest good."

Nick traveled to the "life between lives" dimension. He said he was met by a gentle, wise soul whom he did not know. However, he understood he was greatly loved by this being. He was then taken to a "body selection room" where he saw four distinct bodies. The first was someone who was severely disabled. He shivered and said, "I am not strong enough for this body and experience." The second body was a female. He said, "This lifetime I need to be male," so he rejected that one. The third was a male with high intelligence and no disability. He stated that this third body was too easy, not challenging enough for the specific lessons he desired and needed to learn. The fourth body was the one he chose: small in stature with both physical and mental disabilities. He smiled while he said, "This one is perfect, for it provides me the opportunity to do what I most need to do."

He proceeded to tell me his soul purpose, and the lessons and mission that he needed to accomplish. He also shared that he chose me to be his mom and that I agreed. I knew this was a spiritual truth.

For decades I utilized spiritual hypnosis with clients to help them heal from whatever issue was presenting conflict and stagnation. Hundreds of clients reported that they did in fact choose their parents and for very specific reasons. Their parents, of course, had to agree to this soul contract, for it needs to serve a purpose for everyone's highest good. My clients have shown me that souls travel together lifetime after lifetime. Sometimes we journey to help each other and sometimes to heal the karmic relationship.

I remember experiencing a specific past life regression where I saw myself as a young tribal male who was annoyed that he (I) had to watch over his (my) younger brother. While hunting, I neglected and dismissed my brother to the point that he became severely injured. In that lifetime I felt shame, remorse, and resentment towards him. When I traveled to the life between lives state, I became aware that my son today was my brother in that previous life. I guess I am driven to heal and make up for it now.

This spurred me to check out both our astrological birth charts to see if I could identify any findings related to our purpose of being together again. Sure enough, our soul contract was there in plain sight. Saturn is the planet of responsibility, hard lessons, and limitation or restriction.

Saturn is in my house of children. Hence, "responsibility and hard lessons with a child." Nick's Saturn is in his third house of communication, mental intelligence, analytical ability, practical sensibility, and early education. Again, "restriction and limitation" was revealed in his chart.

Was this our destiny? I believe we all make blueprints, divine plans, before we are born. Sometimes we follow the yellow brick road, and sometimes we take detours. At the end of our present lifetime, I believe the only thing that matters is how much and how well we loved, including ourselves.

At the end of the session, Nick cried as he hugged me. He said, "I get it now."

That was the day a miracle happened because he shifted his thinking and how he perceived himself from that moment on. Nick became excited about making new friends, friends who were like him. That was the day he started to accept and love himself.

What I learned:

- No amount of nagging or wishing is going to change behaviors or beliefs in your kid. Sometimes they have to learn the hard way and figure it out themselves. It's his journey, not yours.

- Astrological natal charts are eye opening. They are not fortunetellers but rather an ancient science that reveals the blueprint a soul chooses for itself in order to learn life lessons and to provide the opportunities to accomplish its divine plan. A birth chart will show potential and challenges related to personality, talents, purpose, lessons, possible vocation, love and marriage, etc. There are free natal charts online, but a good professional astrologer will provide invaluable insight and be able to tell you so much more.

- Your child has all the answers inside. Getting in touch with his/her spiritual nature can create miracles large and small.

- Birds of a feather really do flock together.

- Self-acceptance and self-love matter most, for you need to accept and love yourself before you can attract others who will reciprocate those gifts.

CHAPTER 11

SELF-ADVOCACY:
What We Learned About Self and Helping Others Who Walk in Our Shoes

For many years Nick was in the Division of Developmental Disability (DDD) system, but I didn't know how to use it or what they offered, so I ignored it. Whatever I needed I just did myself. When I think about it now, I have no idea how I did it all while working fulltime. Being a supermom is underrated, undervalued, and insane. It wasn't until my trip to the dentist that my eyes were opened.

Dr. F always asked about Nick. One day when I finally complained and spoke my truth, he said, "Why not call the cerebral palsy center in Edison? I am sure they can tell you where you need to go and who you need to speak to."

Even though my son was diagnosed with cerebral palsy at birth, he overcame it to the point that no one would know he has an extremely mild form of it now. I never thought of reaching out to them. When I contacted them I was given wonderful advice. The woman on the phone told me to contact my son's case manager at DDD and ask to receive the Personal Preference Program (PPP).

PPP is a service that provides in-home support, i.e., meals, cleaning, laundry, hygiene, etc. for DDD clients who live either with the family or in their own apartment. In Nick's case, we definitely needed an aide to help him keep up with basic living chores. He was physically capable but required prompting to get things organized or completed. In fact, we desperately needed this help.

After I called multiple times, my case manager denied access to the PPP program. It wasn't "advertised," and few people actually knew about it. My husband told me that "the loudest voice gets heard," so I wrote to the director of the department and followed up with repeated phone calls. Within a few months, Nick received the PPP help he needed. I wasn't comfortable being so pushy, but I knew we needed it, so I did what I had to do. I have since advised many other parents to receive the help they required by asking for what they wanted.

Nick also learned to advocate for himself at an early age. When he was three, we were standing in a line at the bagel store. They were giving away free mini bagels, and he kept pestering me to get one for him.

I looked at him and said, "If you ask for one, I am sure you will get one."

He squirmed but I remained firm. I wasn't going to cut in line just because my kid was having a bagel obsession. He then said, "Excuse me" to everyone who stood in front of him in order to move up to the counter. When he finally got there, he was so tiny he couldn't see the top of the counter. However, Nick wanted that bagel and somehow made his small voice heard by the clerk. She awarded him the bagel and Nick beamed with pride.

After that day, when I saw my son lacking self-confidence or fearing rejection, I just said, "mini-bagel" and he got the message. This became his signal to "Face Your Fear and Do It Anyway."

Self-advocacy is a huge necessity for a child with special needs because I recognize as his parent that one day I will leave the planet. My kid has to learn to ask for what he needs and now he does.

Nick participates in several self-advocacy groups for people with varying types and levels of disabilities. If he can do it, anyone can.

What I learned:

- Persistence is crucial when advocating.

- Ask parents and agencies to keep referring other contacts until you get the guidance you need.

- Don't take "no" as the only or final answer. Go above the person you are dealing with if you have to.

- Once you learn something, help others to navigate the system too. It feels good to be good.

- Teach your kid how to advocate. It will grow their self-esteem and in the long run help them be more independent.

- Join a parent support or advocacy group. If they don't have one near you, create one like I did.

CHAPTER 12

ADVICE:
What I Learned About Listening and Getting What You Need

Every parent believes they are the "expert" on their child, and I was no exception. I thought I knew everything about what was good and what would or would not work for my son. I was progressive, yes, but also in denial. I had hope and still do but was unable to see my son's future in a realistic way. A friend finally opened my eyes to something I didn't initially want to see, hear or admit: Supplemental Security Income (SSI).

I had many preconceived ideas about what SSI meant. I had heard horror stories about obtaining SSI as well. I'd heard that everyone initially gets declined and that you ultimately had to spend a small fortune on a lawyer to fight for this benefit your child deserves. I remember thinking, "Am I really up for another uphill battle?" I knew my friend was right. I had to acquire this for Nick. Without it, he would not receive Medicaid, which pays for the support services he needed. I had no other choice.

However, I remember thinking, "Let's try a different way, plan B." Most people apply by filling out an application with medical records attached. We decided to get a neuro-psyche evaluation from the Kessler Institute where Christopher Reeves went. Thankfully my husband's insurance paid for the six-hour evaluation, and a thirty-two-page extensive report.

With this in-depth documentation along with the typical medical reports, my son was accepted on the first try. We were overjoyed by this entirely unexpected outcome. In most cases, an attorney suggests that an extensive evaluation is undertaken once your child is rejected.

My family submitted the report first, and we didn't have to fight. Nick has now benefitted from this SSI for many years. However, it's the Medicaid that affords him the benefit of having the necessary supports he needs to live alone with help and to be able to participate in the community.

If I didn't heed the advice from my friend, we still would be doing everything on our own and enabling Nick. I am grateful that I was willing to let go of my ego and control and truly listen. The advice given changed everything for my family and indeed created a magical outcome.

What I learned:

- Talk and listen to your family and friends. They can see what you can't or won't.

- If you don't know what to do, ask for advice.

- Seek out others who have received an outcome you want. Ask how they did it and follow the same steps.

CHAPTER 13

CLARITY:
What I Learned About
"All Your Answers are Within"

Today was a magical day. I picked Nick up early from his apartment to get a haircut prior to meeting his important advocacy group. The timing was perfect since no one was waiting. I thought that odd but recognized it for what it was, a gift.

When we stopped at my house for a quick bite, he said he had a headache. Since he has hydrocephalus, you would think I would get anxious every time he complained about a headache. I don't because I have learned to just go with how I feel and to observe his body language. In my gut I knew he was just tired and had sinus pressure.

Nick needed to have focus, concentration, and initiative at this two-day meeting, so a headache at the outset didn't look promising. I told him to just close his eyes and take three long deep breaths. I figured he would be able to relax, be more calm and feel better. However, his subconscious mind had other plans.

Within seconds after the three breaths, his eyelids fluttered rapidly. He was entering into a trance, so I told him to go down, down, down with the elevator lights in his mind while I counted from 10 down to 1. When the elevator doors opened, I told him that he was in a place where he was supposed to be. He said he was at a dance with a large crowd. The attendees seemed nice, but he did not feel comfortable being there. He listened to his feelings and knew intuitively it was not right for him. I told him then to just go where he needed to on the count from 1 to 5.

Nick said he felt joyful and comfortable because he was with his tribe. I assumed he meant his "birds of a feather," but I was mistaken. He said he was in North Carolina with a group of young adults sitting around him listening to his stories. He said he was 62 and a medicine healer. When I asked if there was anything else he needed to say, he stated that he was proud of his grandson because he was getting married to a woman who was *right* for him. I asked what kind of a woman is "right," and he said the one that calms his soul. He explained that his grandson held a lot of anger and resentment that needed to be softened by the right woman. He met her at a gathering that included a neighboring tribe. This new wife was an assistant to her tribal medicine man, which pleased this 62-year-old medicine healer greatly.

Next I asked Nick to travel through a forest until he saw paths. He said he saw two. I told him they were paths into the future, and, on the count from 1 to 5, he would move deeply down the path of his first choice. Nick saw himself in his mid-40s in an office where he was practicing energy work. He said he loved his work and had been doing it for a while. He was literally moved to tears as he described his soon-to-be wife. He said she was exceptionally compassionate, tender, and held his feet to the fire. He expressed how much fun they had together and said they could talk about anything. She accepted him completely and loved him unconditionally. He started having a conversation with her and expressed his gratitude and deep love for her. It sounded like wedding vows to me. It was really quite beautiful to witness.

I then asked Nick to come back to the forest and travel down the other path. I was so curious to see what this next path held for him. What could possibly top this? However, his subconscious mind showed him something entirely different.

Nick started to say that he felt entirely alone and frightened because he was in an institution for people with dementia. When I asked what happened, he said that he became so angry about not moving forward with his job. I didn't ask him how he ended up in the institution, but he said he had been lonely, depressed, and angry for a very long time. He then said it was because of his sabotaging behaviors over which he never got control. He critically sabotaged himself to the point where institutionalization had to occur. He explained in detail what those behaviors were and felt tremendous shame. I told him to go back to the forest, turn around, and walk towards the cave.

Inside the cave were three beings: Gramps (my dad) and two others. I told him to let the first "other" speak. This was a healing guide named Raphael who said that he worked with many healers on earth. He said he would assist Nick with his own healing and ability to help others if he chose that path.

The next "other" was a young boy named Carl who said he was Nick's future son. Carl said he was ecstatic to reconnect with Nick since they traveled together in many lifetimes. Nick asked him if he, Carl, could help him restore his passion, innocence, and joy. Carl agreed and said it would be his honor since there was so much love between them.

Gramps waited patiently to talk, and, when it was his turn, Gramps was surprisingly firm. He said he was disappointed that Nick was still choosing sabotaging behaviors instead of utilizing his gifts and working toward his life's mission. Gramps became quite loud when he reminded Nick of this, asking him, "Are you here for a season or a reason?" I didn't question the validity of this conversation or vision, because I knew that is exactly what my dad would say to Nick and exactly how. Besides, Nick was trembling with tears coming down his cheeks. Gramps is his idol, and he knew which path Gramps was referring to.

I told him to allow Gramps' energy to meld with his, then Raphael's, then Carl's. I watched how his body deeply relaxed while a beautiful smile came upon his face. He was being divinely embraced and literally felt it.

When I looked at the clock, he had minutes to get to his overnight meeting. I counted him back up from 1 to 10, told him that he would feel terrific in every way when he awakened.

By 10 he opened his eyes and said, "Oh My God! Wow!" He felt mentally alert, emotionally at peace, physically energized, and spiritually so much more aware of his choices. Like I said, a magical day.

What I learned:

- At least on a subconscious level, every person knows how to heal himself or herself. The body, mind, and spirit knows *everything*...and understands how to bring back balance.

- To deeply listen, be fully present and go with the flow.

- There are always choices.

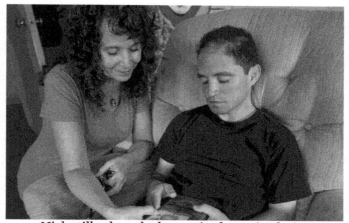

Nick still asks to be hypnotized to gain clarity
and inner truth.

CHAPTER 14

RELATIONSHIP:
What I Learned About Divine Timing

I always knew what kind of man I wanted to marry, but manifesting him at the right time of my life was left to my higher self, not my conscious self. They say that timing is everything, and in this case it was so true.

Giving birth to a very premature infant took all my time and attention. I was oblivious to my own needs let alone anyone else's. The only thing that mattered to me was helping my baby survive and bringing him home. Thank God I was single at the time because I was able to devote everything to the little one who needed me.

My new fulltime job was being a facilitator for infant stimulation and early intervention. Since my baby with cerebral palsy responded to my physical touch, I enrolled in massage school to work on him and provide some income for us. To supplement my income, I taught massage at a local community college.

My husband signed up to be a student in my class a year before we met. When he initially enrolled, the class was full. He decided to leave his money in the college for an entire year to be assured a spot in the following year's offering. When I think about it now, it is so out of character for him to leave his money pending, especially in a class that really didn't interest him much. The stars were aligned for us to find each other when we were *supposed* to meet—one year later.

I was too busy with my son and frankly not emotionally available when he initially signed up. He told me that he went to his father's grave and said, "I am so lonely." A year later we met. Divine perfect timing.

We started out as good friends. We were drastically different and came from dissimilar cultures. We helped each other heal our emotional wounds by listening deeply and accepting each other as we were. Because we were friends, we didn't have to wear masks or pretend to be anybody other than who we were. I learned that he was a kind man, exceptionally devoted to his three children and his mom. When he realized he started having feelings for me, this troubled him because he really didn't want to take on a younger child, especially one with who knows what kind of disabilities later on. But, as he will tell you, "I grew on him."

His kids and his whole Italian family were terrific with Nick and me. However, Nick reacted with jealousy. He found the idea of sharing me with a new man in our life unacceptable and acted out in any way he could. I suppose his goal was to make this man leave us, so he acted out *big time*. It was frustrating for all of us for many years. It is truly amazing that my husband hung in there.

Through the years, we often repeated the same arguments and still do. Initially my husband thought my son was just behaving badly. Even though he knew about all the surgeries and frontal lobe issues, he couldn't wrap his brain around Nick having a true disability. It didn't register with him, especially since my son is so articulate. It took almost two decades after the neuropsychological exam for my husband to truly believe it was not Nick's fault.

Maybe this was a good thing after all. During Nick's childhood and teen years, Dom, my husband, had higher expectations of Nick and therefore *pushed* him towards his potential. Unfortunately, arguments always followed. If I sensed Dom was being too hard on Nick, I would intervene. Dom would get angry and say, "You always take his side." It's true that mostly I did when I saw or felt Nick's self-esteem being squashed.

The stress and fighting were crushing our marriage. I remember one day when I was feeling so frustrated and wanting to call it quits, I prayed. I asked for guidance. That day I walked in a forest where I had never been before. As I walked, I was still struggling with my emotions and thoughts when I became dumbfounded by what I saw. At the end of the path was a clearing. In the center of the clearing was a massive rock shaped like a heart. I was so startled when I saw this that it abruptly stopped my *stinking thinking.*

I asked, "What does this mean?" At that moment I looked up at the sky and saw two beautiful white birds flying together and in sync. I knew then that my husband was my great love and that I needed to change my thoughts immediately.

I realized that Dom's insistence on getting Nick to "man up" was a blessing because my son gained invaluable character lessons in courage, integrity, resilience, and honor.

Another realization occurred one day when we were visiting Nick at Maplebrook, the post-secondary sleepaway school.

Another mom approached me and said, "Your husband is not your son's biological father, is he?" When I told her she was correct, she said with a straight, intense expression, "He must really love you."

To this day I have no idea if she was referring to Nick's behavioral problems at the time or insinuating that a stepdad would never stay. What I do know is that Dom did stay and loves both of us with all his stoic goodness and commitment.

Perhaps our love connection was helped by our taking vacations without Nick. We needed our alone time to rekindle romance and the spark that kept us together.

In the beginning my parents were able to babysit so we could get away. One time I asked a friend to watch him and our dog at their house. They loved taking care of Nick but hated the dog, who destroyed their home. When my parents could no longer help us, I created a scheduling chart with time slots and dates and emailed it to my friends to ask if they were willing to help me by either calling or stopping over to check on Nick while we were away. I had five girlfriends who stepped up to the plate and scheduled themselves in the chart. I was grateful and Nick was thrilled with all the attention.

When Nick moved out of our home and into his own apartment (a desperate move for all of us), Dom and I were finally able to enjoy doing what most husbands and wives do. (Note: Nick had supports in place to be able to live independently.) We scheduled date night on Thursday nights and still make an effort to go out with other married friends. I've noticed that we are more attentive and affectionate to one another when we are around another couple. It subconsciously influences us to be more of a couple ourselves.

Recently I looked over both Dom's and my astrological natal charts to see if I could gain insight. I was delighted to see what I suspected all along. The 7th house is marriage and partnerships. In one's own birth chart, the planet that rules the 7th house will tell you what type of partner you will attract. Capricorn was in mine, telling me that I would attract a more mature person who was loyal, supportive and who has high standards. Capricorn gives a certain sense of responsibility and patience in one's relationship and invites a partner who makes you feel safe. That describes Dom! Ironically he has Capricorn in his 7th house too. Like attracts like, so we are mirror images of each other with respect to how we love. Everything I love about him I find in myself. Our coupling helps us to learn the lessons in relationship that we both need to understand. I find this extraordinary.

Nick too desires a great love. We all do. It is a basic human need to love and be loved. Connection is so vital—like the air we breathe. Unfortunately, he still hasn't made that connection and it bothers him greatly.

At one point he turned to online chat rooms and phone chat lines, which became addictive and dangerous. He now realizes that scams and predators search out victims who are easy prey.

Nick had to learn the hard way. I have always tried to encourage him to meet someone terrific the old-fashioned way: through work, being involved with outside activities that he enjoys, and possibly finding a new *friend* through a current one.

I ordered the PEERS social skills workbook to help him with his impulsivity and differentiating between acquaintance, friend, and possible romantic partner. We need more practice but the workbook is terrific.

I also bought him all kinds of dating dos and don'ts and social etiquette books. Asking my brother to step in to be a dating coach was also good. So was a men's support group.

Nick has no problem initiating and asking a woman out. He doesn't fear rejection, but he is often dismissed because of his short stature. There is definitely a big prejudice against short men. Unfortunately, another battle for Nick to climb.

A few weeks ago, Nick was feeling a little down. I asked if he wanted clarity. He definitely said "yes," so I initiated spiritual hypnosis again. Although I am psychic, sometimes too psychic for Nick's taste, I didn't want to simply *give* him the answers, so I chose to do spiritual hypnosis. This highly experiential modality enables him to explore his own higher mind to receive his own answers. It's much more powerful to "know what you know" on a deep gut level, which was what he needed in the moment.

Again, he easily went into a deep trance within a few minutes. He said he felt a presence of an exceptionally loving and compassionate woman inches from his face. I asked him if it was a spirit guide or a loved one who had crossed over. He instinctively knew that it was a soul mate who was waiting for him to "step up to the plate" so they could be together. She told him she would not come into his life before he was ready. She showed him what he needed to do and let go of in order to mature and attract her. The divine timing then was dependent on his choices moving forward.

It reminded me about the divine timing of how Dom and I met. I believe there is a lid for every pot. Now it is up to Nick. If he wants her badly enough, he will manifest this beautiful relationship when he consciously chooses to love himself completely. For how can we completely love another if we don't fully love ourselves first? Like attracts like, but Love attracts Love.

What I learned:

- We all have a relationship blueprint before we are born. We also have free will. Whatever we choose with our thoughts and actions will manifest in time in exact reference to those thoughts and actions.

- Forgiving, letting go, and rekindling is worth the energy.

- As my mom used to say regarding my husband, "Just remember his good points."

- There is someone for everyone. I truly believe this. A Buddhist saying goes, "When the student is ready, the teacher appears." Well, when the person is ready, the *right one* appears.

My husband Dom and I – August 2020

CHAPTER 15

SELF–CARE:
What I Learned About Being Kind to Self and How to Release My Own Negative Emotions

Every parent knows how crappy it is when you are sick and have to tend to your demanding child through no fault of his own. You reach a point when you feel sick and tired of being sick and tired. At this stage when you hit rock bottom, you beg and plead to whomever is listening upstairs in heaven to please send help.

My awareness came when I put on 50 extra pounds and was told that I had Chronic Fatigue Syndrome due to prolonged stress. I didn't need a doctor to tell me about chronic stress. What I did need was a good kick in the butt to turn my whole life around, and that meant putting me first for a change.

I created a strategic wellness plan that

incorporated all my needs: physical, emotional, mental, and spiritual. I first tackled the physical, which I thought would be the easiest. I stopped going through drive-through fast food and began a regimen that was suggested for my body type, using *Dr. Abravanel's Body Type Diet and Lifetime Nutrition Plan*. Dr. Elliot Abravanel's book includes an in-depth assessment which tailors a specific food plan according to your type.

While dieting, I walked on the treadmill and imagined a detailed scenario of my ideal weight as if it already had happened. I visualized trying on my wedding dress and noticing that it was too large for my slim body. I felt the fabric and was able to grab a handful on either side. I also experienced the joy of the dress being too big as I looked into the mirror.

This visualization actually materialized, and I lost the 50 pounds in four months and have kept it off for 14 years. Since I discovered a fantastic YouTube fitness walking expert named Leslie Sansone, I go to the gym sporadically now. She offers many options from 15 minutes to 48-minute sessions. You can always opt in to her site to receive more programs and guidance.

In addition, I visited a functional medicine doctor who discovers and treats the cause and not the symptoms of "dis-ease." I learned what foods heal me and which ones hurt me. Once you've been on the program for a while, it is really obvious when you eat something that doesn't work for your specific bodily needs. Major eye opener!

After this change in lifestyle and eating, I felt way more energy and more empowered. Fatigue? What fatigue? My thoughts combined with action and strong emotional feeling healed my physical body.

Emotional healing was an ongoing process because of the constant triggers in my life. I learned to recognize the pressure building in my body before it escalated into *whatever*. I learned to speak my truth with calmness. I talked with various therapists through the years. Some were helpful and some were just okay. I began to listen to my feelings and disconnect or detach from work, family, or friends when I needed downtime or a mental health day. I acknowledged when I needed nurturing, so I would book a massage or call my mom. Sometimes I would ask my friend to schedule a girls' weekend. This was amazingly therapeutic thanks to all the laughter and time away from my routine. So was meditation with instrumental, calming music.

Mental needs were addressed with what stimulated me. As long as I can remember, anything related to metaphysics and healing turned the lights on in my brain. I would read, research, attend classes, and study the many subjects that interested me. For example, I studied and received certifications in all kinds of massage and energy healing techniques, psychic/mediumship development, spirit art, reiki, shamanism, color therapy, theory and image consulting, and, of course, clinical and spiritual hypnosis, which included past lives and the life between lives state. This became a primary focus which I performed in private practice for decades. All these different modalities that interested me were practiced on my son. We discovered what worked and found the ones that served his needs best. It made a huge difference in our journey.

I also found a reasonable water color teacher in my town. She provided the supplies, and all I had to do was show up. I didn't think I could paint. I was wrong. I allowed myself to just sketch what interested me and then paint it. It didn't matter to me that some people judged my work and didn't like it. What counted was how I felt while I was in the process of creating. For two hours each week, time stood still. I was absorbed and mesmerized by the colors, brushstrokes, and the moment. It was so therapeutic.

I stopped when my time was needed by my parents and my son, but I still continued to paint on a small water color pad with cheap paints and brushes. It was the creative journey that I found meaningful, not the finished product.

A few months ago I took part in a "process painting" group. I never heard of this before and it is so freeing. No structure or instruction. You have a large canvas and just paint with acrylics based on how you are feeling. It is cool and insightful after the process is completed. Again, all the supplies were provided, and I just had to show up.

Spiritual needs were also fulfilled by reconnecting to God on a personal level. I am not religious but I am extremely spiritual. I believe God and our unseen helpers invite us all to evolve and let go of despair when we are open to receive help by asking. God and/or guides (I believe we each have many) became my confidants. I would talk or get guidance by meditating, asking a question, and waiting for a sign or answer. Sometimes I would be in a place where I simply could not shut down and quiet my mind, so I asked for help with my inner mind and just waited to receive.

Sometimes the answer would be delivered instantaneously in a thought or a sign on the road that grabbed my attention. Other times I just needed to trust that the answer would find me. I just needed to be patient and *trust*. Faith has carried me far.

Other useful tools I have used include self-hypnosis, spiritual hypnosis from a colleague, guidance from an Akashic records practitioner, intuitive self-readings from oracle cards, dowsing with a pendulum, and utilizing the services of a reputable psychic/medium. Mostly, I feel the guidance in my solar plexus (gut) and hear it internally. Again, I trust because I acknowledge *how I feel* and *what I know*, and the guidance has never let me down.

Regarding stress: I was in the sandwich generation for a few years before both of my parents passed. In their golden age years, Dad became physically incapacitated while my mom became mentally disabled with Alzheimer's. I was in and out of emergency rooms with both of them. One late night I was in the ER with my son when I received a call that my dad went to the ER in a different county. Talk about stress! I had to practice what I preached. I allowed myself the luxury of a few seconds to feel my panic, then took some slow, deep breaths to get level headed and stimulate the vagus nerve response. I then asked God to intervene and called on guides and angels to step up. They all survived at the time and so did I.

Afterwards, I took a day to myself (again by asking others to help) in order to get my equilibrium back. I still take those days when I need them. I recognize my worth now.

What I learned:

- I matter too.

- Self-care is a necessity in any form it takes.

- Ask your spouse, family, friends, or an agency to help you when you need a break.

- Acknowledge your needs in all aspects of life. Reach out beyond your comfort zone to what feels good, sounds good, or is good. It's true that "if there's a will, there's a way."

CHAPTER 16

INDEPENDENCE:
What I Learned About Living Alone and With Supports

In order to save my marriage and sanity, I became the mama bird that pushes baby bird out of the nest in order for it to fly.

My son was in his mid-20s when I realized that he could no longer live in the same house with me if we wanted all our relationships to remain intact. Besides, we were getting older and I knew I had to find adequate placement for him before I died. This is when our hunt for a safe, secure, and affordable apartment began.

My son was on the DDD waiting list for a long time for a group home. The wait was crazy long, and we couldn't sit by any longer. I looked into alternative housing options. Some offered built-in supports and social outings but were unaffordable for us at $60k plus per year. We also knew that the state would not pay for such luxury facilities.

One day my husband found an article in the paper about the Costello Complex located in Middlesex County, New Jersey. It was specifically built for people with all kinds of disabilities, low income, and a few seniors. A county-run shuttle bus ran to the facility Monday through Friday. They offered some activities and took SSI and DDD vouchers. We loved it, he loved it, and, yes, there was a two-year waiting list. Eventually his number came up and he moved into a one-bedroom apartment.

This is not a group home but rather an apartment that offers independent living. It was my job to find a direct support person to assist him with daily chores, meal planning, cooking, etc. Nick didn't need a maid; he needed an Annie Sullivan, someone to show him how to organize his surroundings and live as independently as possible.

Initially I sent out a massive email blast, and the person I hired was exactly the teacher/coach/mentor required. They fought a lot, but he learned a great deal too. She would visit him at 6:00 a.m. every Monday through Friday and stay until 8:30 a.m. She made sure he was following his chore chart, doing the actual work, and taking his meds. They planned meals, cooked together, and discussed issues and/or desires. She used a timer to keep him on target and referred to the many posters and reminders she created that were displayed everywhere in his apartment. We ALL needed her and she was a Godsend. Prior to her arrival his apartment was in complete chaos on a daily basis. It took seven years for him to realize how structure and an orderly, clean apartment does wonders for his emotional, mental, physical, and spiritual health.

She has since moved on. I now have taken on some of her duties as his PPP provider (Personal Preference Plan) with additional help from an agency aide that comes one hour in the mornings Monday through Friday and a different aide two nights a week for two hours each night. His budget from DDD pays for these direct support people (DSP).

In addition, Nick now relies on Uber for other transportation, which is also subsidized through his DDD budget. He heavily advocated for this as his Partners in Policy Training Project, and amazingly it has come to fruition. Transportation is such a huge issue in our state (probably in most states). How gratifying to know that one can really make a difference that helps all.

Social involvement was initially an issue. All the years of rejection kept him isolated in his apartment. He would reach out to strangers in online chatrooms, thinking he was safe and secure. Wrong! After much intervention, we had to take away his computer and internet service. Then he started getting on phone chatrooms. That was a big mistake with even more frustration for all of us. This became an addiction and obsession because his need to connect was so vitally intense.

I was on a mission to get him involved socially outside of his apartment. He worked on Tuesday, Wednesday, and Thursday, so those days were covered. We got him involved with Friday night social clubs, Disability Allies programming on Saturday, Taekwondo in the evening, a Unitarian church on Sundays, and a NAMI program for young adults biweekly on Sundays. Now he is also involved in three or four different advocacy groups, including a recent volunteer program to enhance independence for people with disabilities.

He is busy and I am grateful. He has made friends and I am grateful. He has matured and I am grateful. He has become much more independent and I am grateful. Yes, I am still his taxi many days, but I don't mind because I am deeply thankful.

At the beginning of his independent living journey, I was scared. I didn't let him know, but the truth was I sometimes would panic if he didn't answer the phone. My husband would settle me down and say, "If something happened you would receive a call." He's right, of course, but your imagination can run wild if you let it. Now, most days I feel that "no news is good news."

What I learned:

- Let your kid grow up no matter how hard it is to let them go.

- They are so much more capable if you give them a chance to prove it.

- Ask the universe to send you the Annie Sullivan or Mary Poppins that they need to help them grow independently.

- Be patient but take heart and be strong. You are not alone.

CHAPTER 17

PARENTS SERVING PARENTS:
What I Learned About Supporting
Each Other and Giving Back

As I mentioned earlier in the book, I approached two other moms to start our own support group when the one we belonged to dissolved. The former one was formal. This new one was much more informal, which enabled us to get deeply personal about our "issues" and help one another with suggestions and options that we would not have thought about ourselves. Although invited speakers to address our group, we benefited most from being able to share and support each other because, as parents of special needs children know, we walk in each other's shoes.

We invited our adult children to join us for one meeting to take a wonderful assessment for living independently that was developed by a Canadian agency. I discovered it online and disseminated it to our members prior to the meeting. Everyone thought it was a good idea for the adult kids to do the assessment and to meet and socialize as well. The moms filled out the assessment too, but it was important for the young adults to independently take the test to get a realistic view of how really ready to live independently they actually were.

This Canadian agency has so many other valuable resources. Check out their website at https://connectability.ca/. Look through the site to find the Steps to Independence assessment if you feel this would be helpful to you as well.

We decided to include our young adults for the next couple of meetings. They wanted to get together outside the moms' group and planned a lunch where they would meal plan, shop, and cook. They selected a Mexican theme and divided up the responsibilities as to who would make which course. They arranged to discuss it further in a Facebook meeting. Unfortunately, the coronavirus has stopped the initial plans for now. However, the young adults felt empowered and gained a sense of belonging because they were making all the decisions and everyone was included in the process.

At one meeting, one of the young adults expressed her concern about being bullied and not standing up for herself. She gave us a recent example, and her mom and I started acting out the scenario. It was intense and pretty accurate as to what transpired and the feelings it induced. Next, her mom and I improvised another scene where she became empowered and learned how to forgive and move on. The daughter not only saw the lesson easily but demonstrated it to all in the room when she chose to act out a new scenario herself. It was a wonderful experience for everyone present. It just kind of happened, and it was magical to see the shift not just in her but in everyone.

We have come to rely on each other for updates, news, and developments. We email blast whatever we feel is important and may benefit one another.

In addition, I belong to two special needs parenting groups on Facebook. I searched for special needs parent groups in New Jersey, and this is what I found: (1) NJ Special Needs Resources, (2) NJ Special Needs Connections. Someone posts a question and the responses are many. I have learned so much from these other parents. Even now I have come to realize there is so much out there that I still don't know: resources, new clinical studies, new tools, and developments.

Prior to reaching out to other parents who understood, I felt alone and frustrated many days. My husband kept saying, "Join a group so you can see what they are doing." I resisted because I was working fulltime and exhausted from doing my other caretaking duties plus my metaphysical business. I felt I didn't have the energy or the time. Big mistake!

What I learned:

- Reach out of your comfort zone and find others like you who need support and can be supported by you. Don't wait. Seek. Someone has answers you probably didn't even know you needed.

- If you discover or learn something that works for you, share it. It feels good to help someone else.

- Emotional support comes in all different forms. Sometimes it's a smile. Perhaps even a hug. Our spirit needs to know we are understood and not alone.

- Be visible, not shy. Post your questions. You will probably be pleasantly surprised.

CHAPTER 18

THE FUTURE:
What I Learned About Help
When I Am No Longer on the Planet

I f there ever was an issue that kept me up at night, this one was probably the biggest. As baby boomers, my husband and I realized we needed to get educated about what's out there and make a plan. We were behaving like ostriches and didn't really want to deal with it, but we had to.

During one of the mom support group meetings, I learned about special needs trusts which protect your child's benefits while providing supplemental funding for other things besides shelter and food. There are two kinds of trusts: first person and third person. It is vital to receive sound advice from an estate lawyer who specializes in these kinds of trusts. The attorney will look over your child's needs and income (including the inheritance from you) and then will advise you as to which trust is better. Most important is deciding who will administer the trust once you leave the planet. This is the key person you identify as the "guardian" to manage the finances. In my case I have my brothers and nephews to take care of this should something happen to my husband and me. A team approach is best. Whoever has the biggest connection and loves your kid the most makes the best team leader, which is also the person who makes the most important decisions.

If you do not have a family member you can count on, there are other possibilities. You can hire a representative payee to handle money management as well as providing protection from financial victimization or abuse. I know of two such payees in New Jersey: Planned Lifetime Assistance Network of NJ, Inc. (http://plannj.org) and Community Access Unlimited (http://caunj.org).

Other options you may want to consider include Pooled Trusts and ABLE Accounts. A good special needs attorney or special needs planner will be able to advise you as to which works best for your situation. You may be able to receive a terrific recommendation from http://specialneedsanswers.com or by asking other parents if they have a trust set up for their child and if they felt their attorney was competent and had their child's best interest uppermost in mind.

Another option is to call the law school in your state and speak to the Secretary of Estate Law. The secretary of the department will give you her opinion based on factors which she will not disclose to you. She knows which faculty member is current with the changing laws and who advocates for special needs planning. Once you get referrals, compare prices and feedback. You will know in your heart who works best for your needs.

Another area to address with your child is death and how to handle grief. Preparing for an emotional fallout is critical. My son and I discussed mine and his dad's death a lot. We told him this was the reason we are so firm about him becoming independent. He got this message on an intellectual level but didn't really experience loss until both his beloved grandparents passed. He was familiar with the afterlife communication from the countless sessions of spiritual hypnosis and hearing decades of stories from me and my friends. It's one thing to hear it and another to experience it personally. It is the personal experience of communication with loved ones who have passed either through mediumship, spiritual hypnosis, dreams, or signs that eases the pain, brings comfort, and makes you a true believer.

The day my Dad died Nick found a shiny penny in the car below his feet and then another one on the front step as he approached it. I reminded him of the phrase "pennies from heaven" and told him that it was a sign that

Gramps would always be with him. Two days later was the Shiva. It's the Jewish version of a wake. My son came down the stairs dressed in his suit but squirming. He looked like he had ants in his pants. By the time he got downstairs, he flung off his shoe and out rolled a shiny penny. He burst into laughter and said, "Gramps, you are crazy funny!"

Another time we were in the car together driving down a country road in the winter and wondering what we should have for dinner. I said, "What would Gramps want?" All of a sudden we both smelled Chinese food. We were in shock and cracked up because my dad loved Chinese food and that was his final request hours before he passed.

Three months after my dad died, I was driving on the Garden State Parkway. It was early in the morning on a Sunday, so there were few cars on the road. Trucks are not allowed on the parkway, so when I saw one speeding up behind me looking like it would kiss my bumper I got really annoyed. As I was watching in the rearview mirror, I was thinking, "Mom is looking like she will pass soon too. I don't know if I am strong enough to handle another void."

When the truck passed me on my right, I couldn't help but look to see who the obnoxious driver was. I never did get a view of the driver because my eyes were distracted by what I saw on the side of the truck. In big lettering was my dad's name, ELLIOTT, with a starburst over the last "t." I was stunned. Then I realized what was playing on the radio, "Calling All Angels."

I burst into tears and thanked my Dad for the obvious sign of his continued presence in our lives. I distinctly heard him say, "What Void?" and then he laughed.

Thomas John, the psychic medium of the Lifetime TV series *Seatbelt Psychic*, was hosting an educational workshop for three days in Lily Dale, New York. It was an eight-hour drive from where we lived, but after seeing the show I had to go. There were hundreds of people in attendance. He did tremendously skilled readings on Friday and announced that Saturday was for psychic mediumship development. We were told that he would do no readings that day since it would be jam-packed with exercises and learning. In the last ten minutes left, Thomas John paused from his class, locked eyes with me, pointed at me and said, "Elliott."

I jumped out of my seat and screamed "Yes!"

He then proceeded to tell me the most accurate things about my dad and gave me a vital message I needed to hear.

He said, "Your dad says that you are correct in your belief that your mother understands what you say to her. She just can't express herself, but she completely knows who you are and what you say to her."

This was huge for me, for my mom was in the advanced stages of Alzheimer's. I kept on insisting that her receptive language was intact even though her expressive language was gone. My brothers and husband always doubted but I knew, and my Dad confirmed what I believed all along. Mom passed three weeks later. I shared all of these visitations from my dad with Nick. He was comforted greatly and knew in his heart that his beloved grandmother was birthed back into spirit on the arm of his dearest Gramps.

What I learned:

- Plan before your child turns 18.

- While you are still alive, get your child set up in a living arrangement with supports away from home.

- Consider creating a small business venture with other parents, i.e., "Popcorn for the People," so your kid can have secure employment.

- Put workplace assistance in place with a job coach. The Division of Vocational Rehabilitation or Easter Seals is a good place to start.

- Enroll your child in programs that promote life progress instead of busywork. Disability Allies in Central New Jersey is an example, or you can hire a Special Needs Life Coach to help you find something appropriate in your area.

- Have the hard talk about loss. It's necessary.

- Find a good psychic medium if you are feeling the loss of your mentor and support on this special needs journey. Both of my parents were mentors to Nick and me. A good medium will confirm their continued existence by communicating they are with you during current happenings in your life now. This is profoundly comforting and healing. I saw how my son's grief and energy shifted once he truly knew in his heart they were still with him, protecting and guiding him as guardian angels.

- Share your personal story with your child, for they trust and learn from us. Besides, you are his/her hero and always will be.

CHAPTER 19

INSIGHT:
What I learned So Far about the Five Questions

In the introduction to this book, I shared five questions and stated, "Perhaps you will also gain answers to the following questions that might stir in your mind." I've described how I did it and now would like to summarize my findings for deeper clarity. Hopefully you will find this helpful.

- *How do I release frustration, anger, and grief in order to feel alive and experience a sense of freedom?* I go within to meditate or pray by closing my door and respecting my need for solitude. I ask for help from others to give me an ear, a hug, or a break. I book a massage, paint, or schedule a psychic reading or healing session. Sometimes I walk in the woods or just sit in the sun. I treasure my needs and am grateful that I can do this. I allow myself a pity party but only for a short time. I am aware of the effect negative thinking, feeling, and perception have on my physical body, so I address whatever I'm feeling in as much of a positive way as I can. Laughter helps a lot, but love, especially self-love, matters most.

- *How do I heal my relationships?* I have come to let go of my ego and of the desire to be right by listening *deeply*. When another person feels "heard," they are willing to lower their guard and have a heart-to-heart talk. My family and I many times disagree, but we have come to understand that we are all entitled to our own opinions. There is a powerful Hawaiian Ho'oponopono healing prayer that I repeat when I need to restore balance and love in our family dynamics. Once my mind and emotions are quiet, I visualize the person I am struggling with. Then I humbly state, "I love you; I am sorry; forgive me; thank you."

This simple phrase is repeated for however long I feel I need to do it. It's profound because it really works. More powerful is the ability to let go of my ego, look the person in the eye and sincerely say, "I am sorry that I hurt you. I love you and it is never my intention to hurt you."

These statements are obvious to everyone

except at times to our own egos. It's wonderful when everyone feels better.

In addition, there have been many times that I have wrestled with my husband to sit on his lap while he is furious with me. I knew if I could get him to crack a smile at the absurdity, he would lower his guard so we could talk. With my son, if he was really angry I would give him "magic water" to break the emotional trigger, then either try to get him to talk out his feelings or laugh. Laughter and honest communication is what helped us.

- *How do I recapture joy?* Oh, this was a tough one to learn at first. When you are feeling physically and emotionally exhausted and frustrated beyond belief, you can't possibly imagine feeling joy let alone contentment. Here's the definition of joy from www.alleydog.com: "Joy is an emotion comprised of feelings of happiness, contentment, and harmony. It differs from general happiness in that it is not caused by a particular event but comes from within the individual ... Joy is a generalized feeling that comes from the person." The key phrase is "comes from within." That is why I cherished my alone time to do creative projects, stimulate my mind, and enjoy occasions spent with my friends and extended family. Vacations with my husband were essential as well. I would schedule this alone time into my calendar and ask others to help out with

Nick. I made it work because I was entitled to joy too.

- *Why me?* The only real thing I can say about this comes from a spiritual truth you awaken to regarding your divine plan. The *aha* moment that comes when you realize that you wrote your own blueprint or soul plan before you were born. You composed specific lessons and opportunities to enhance and challenge your soul growth. You may ask, why my child then? Perhaps your child chose his/her specific challenges to help you learn something that you needed to understand. I know my son chose his body and his disabilities for his specific lessons and purpose as well as to accelerate mine and his dad's growth. From my spiritual work with clients, I became aware that souls travel together lifetime after lifetime. This makes sense to me, especially since we all have to agree to each other's soul plans and make soul contracts. Even Shakespeare said, "All the world's a stage, and all the men and women merely players. They have their exits and their entrances; And one man in his time plays many parts." I believe he meant time as "lifetimes."

- *What's my purpose?* I believe this ties in to "Why me?" Your trials and tribulations from the past prepare you for a life that makes a difference. But your influence reaches beyond your inner circle. Others who have similar circumstances could be helped and find comfort by modeling you. In essence you are leaving a legacy of hope. Your incredible experiences go towards helping and healing others who come after you as surely as your past help you now. You know how others feel and think. You know because you can empathize. You *get it* on all levels. We are all here for a reason. What is your reason?

I encourage you to do what brings you joy. There's that word again. Joy is like love when you first experience that chemical high. There is no effort; it just happens. You are in your joy when you detach from the external and become present with yourself in an act of self-love. It's what I call a magical moment. It is when time stands still, and you are doing or being in your heart's desire.

To my fellow parents, my wish for you is that you take a curious journey out of your comfort zone. You never know what can happen unless you try. If you received a little gem from this book, please share what you learned with other parents. We are on this journey together.

God bless you!

Thirty-five years later. August 2020, my son Nick and I.

EPILOGUE

BY NICHOLAS TAUBENSLAG

During my childhood, I was frustrated with kids teasing me and calling me "Shorty." I never was able to fit into the mainstream crowd. I was never included in people's social gatherings outside of lunch period. As a result, I became angry and had a huge chip on my shoulder, which only caused them to shun me even more. I would lash out, even toward the people who were closest to me. There were times where I would act out at people in fits of anger for no apparent reason. I realize now that this behavior only kept me even more trapped in my inner prison. At that time, I thought I needed to protect myself from being emotionally abused by acting out in anger. Truth be told, all I ever wanted was to feel loved and accepted by my own peers.

However, the only real times I felt accepted

and loved were in drama club and summer theater. Without that humble and fun beginning, I don't know where I'd be today. I tried to reconnect to these groups in recent years, but I am not included in their gatherings. They all have their own families and lives now, so it's like I'm out of sight and mind. From this situation I've learned to forgive and move forward with my life. I've realized that it's pointless to dwell in frustration, anger, fear, grief, and sadness. It's extremely important to surround myself with people who will love and cherish me for who I really am on the inside.

There were rare instances of connection with some people, but they were really short-lived. For example, my one childhood best friend and I used to laugh and pal around a lot when we were younger. We had such a close brotherly bond and now we don't anymore. I miss going four-wheeling, having sleepovers, going to his parents' vacation home in the Poconos, and playing video games with him. Ever since I hurt him in some way, he has distanced himself from me. I realize now that it's useless to try and repair old relationships.

When I lost my precious grandmother and grandfather, it really took a lot out of me. But knowing that I am a valued and loved member of the Taubenslag family keeps me going. I've lost a lot of potential friendships over the years, which is most likely due to the chip on my shoulder that I had as a child. I've grown a lot from it.

With regards to healing relationships that matter most to me, I think of my family. When I have heart-to-heart conversations with my dad, I believe it heals both of us. I know he means well and is coming from a place of unconditional love and understanding. We have had great bonding moments which have made me feel better about myself and our relationship. I really appreciate those times because it has shown me that we can build a close bond.

Reflecting back on the twelve principles of the Scout Law, which state, "A scout is trustworthy, loyal, helpful, friendly, courteous, kind, obedient, cheerful, thrifty, brave, clean, and reverent," I've come to realize that my terrific role model of a father emulates all these qualities on a constant, daily basis. I recognize that these principles are extremely important to mirror in the relationships I have now so they are of pure intention and not based on negative, ruminating thoughts.

After reflecting on what I've done wrong in past relationships, I realize now that it's useless to dwell on it. A dear friend of mine illustrates this point perfectly when he stated to me, "Rather than dwell on past relationships that have already been burned, please focus on the relationships with the people who really value, respect, and want to spend quality time with you because it's those relationships that will cultivate the most inner growth in yourself than you can possibly imagine." This beautiful quote is a refocusing tool for me when I get stuck ruminating negative thoughts. When I am humble and pray, it shows a light in the darkness.

I recapture my joy by remembering the good times I had with others and by listening to uplifting music. I bring back my joy by focusing on cultivating more wholesome relationships with the people that are closest to me and those who value, respect, and really want to spend quality time with me. By focusing on all this, I can create a life for myself that has meaning, purpose, and pure relationships.

I struggled with questioning why I have conditions like hydrocephalus, sensitive lungs during the change of seasons, shortness of stature, and social exclusion, for a long time. All this questioning and pondering negativity brought anger, resentment, feelings of being invisible, and fear. I became angry due to my so-called peers not wanting to acknowledge and accept me. I became resentful of the harsh judgments I received and, in turn, put those back on my mainstreamed peers. As a result, I felt invisible, like no one was really seeing what I could bring to the table, and I felt really isolated.

Many modalities really helped me move forward and release a lot of negative feeling and thinking, including anger management workshops, the Mankind Project, breath work, and much more.

Anger management workshops helped by giving me tools to acknowledge and work through all that pent-up emotion. Utilizing breath work enabled me to fully express those emotions. In doing so, I felt calm and stable. The Mankind Project took it a step further by using psycho-drama so I was able to act out specific traumatic scenes and work through those feelings. I highly recommend the Mankind Project for other men. It is based on supporting each other with unconditional love and tremendous compassion. It is really a rewarding experience in which men who barely know one another come together and help each other work through any type of male issue you can imagine.

Another alternative modality that helped me was working with oracle decks for self-exploration. In doing so, I gained moments of self-actualization that helped and strengthened my emotional morale and self-esteem.

One of the most impactful alternative methods was becoming attuned to the White Light Reiki Energy frequency. It has given me the ability to heal my physical, mental, emotional, and spiritual body on a deep level. I really enjoy doing the energy work. I feel it has given me a tool to keep myself calm, cool, and focused.

Most importantly, I'd like to honor and sincerely thank my resourceful mother who is always working tirelessly by researching and implementing new ways to help me move forward in all areas of my life. Without her help all this self-growth would have never been possible.

I discovered my life purpose through my mom's research about New Jersey Partners in Policymaking and her suggesting that I fill out the application. This national educational advocacy program is dear to me. The New Jersey chapter is sponsored by the Boggs Center of Rutgers. Each year twenty-five individuals are selected from the Intellectual Developmental Disabled Community or their caregivers to learn how to advocate on local, state, and federal levels. It takes a lot of hard work, tremendous focus, and a mentality that you are part of something greater than yourself. It's exhausting, yet if you push through and really remain focused, you can reap amazing opportunities in the future.

Since graduating from New Jersey Partners in Policymaking, I have become a passionate advocate passionate about advocating for the expansion of transportation options for the disabled community. The action plan I worked on was forming a quadruple partnership among the Division of Developmental Disabilities, Attain and Gain, Uber, and the DDD clients. Attain & Gain is the financial intermediary between DDD and Uber. This partnership allows for the DDD clients themselves to become more self-sufficient by not having to rely on friends and family to take them places.

Here is how the process works. The DDD client goes onto the Attain and Gain website and creates an account. The account information gets sent to their Support Coordinator to get approved to be part of their DDD budget. Once it is approved, the client then downloads the Uber app onto their cell phone and links the Attain and Gain account to their Uber app. As a result, the DDD client can be more independent and have peace of mind knowing their transportation needs are met.

I have come to realize that selflessly serving others with kindness, love, and compassion is truly my life purpose. This has given me a brand new lease on life.

It's important for everyone to awaken to their own life purpose whatever that may be because it helps to reframe the *selfish ego* mindset into the *selfless service* mindset. To illustrate my point, I would like to quote my grandfather who once asked me, "Are you here for a season, or are you here for a reason? If you are here for a season, you are like a leaf on a tree that just blows away in the wind, and its time is over; it is forgotten. However, if you're here for a reason, then you are here for a purpose, to make a difference in the world through kindness, love, and compassion."

What this quote really means to me is you need to find something you are passionate about and work towards leaving a lasting legacy behind for generations to come.

In closing, I urge you to always keep this

question in the back of your minds: How may I serve the greater good of mankind and really make a difference in others' lives? By doing so, the world will become a better place.

Nicholas Taubenslag, Self-Advocate for
People with Disabilities

ABOUT THE AUTHOR

Debra Taubenslag, *The Transformational Mentor,* facilitates transformational change by awakening parents of special needs children to their highest potential and calling utilizing spiritual hypnosis, healing, and intuitive guidance. She specializes in helping her clients recapture balance, joy, and creativity by acknowledging and reclaiming their spiritual selves in order to live a meaningful, and purposeful life.

Born in New Brunswick, New Jersey, Debra Taubenslag holds a Doctorate in Clinical Hypnosis, and two teaching degrees; Special Education, and Speech and Theater. She has also been on the faculty at a community college as a teacher of Hypnosis and Massage Therapy.

Debra has gained much experience in the area of public speaking and has presented worldwide presentations to corporations, holistic centers and hypnosis conventions. She is the author of two books. Her new release, *NO STONE UNTURNED: How My Special Needs Child and I Transformed Against All Odds,* was written to help caregivers like herself find meaning and thrive. Her first book, *Not Crazy Just Enlightened* published in 2000, resulted in a national nineteen-city book tour where she educated the public by conducting metaphysical stage hypnosis shows.

Through the development of her own

spiritual awareness, her mission is to help people discover their true purpose, why they are here, and what they need to accomplish.

If you are inspired to connect with Debra, visit her website at **www.debrataubenslag.com.**

Note from the author: One more thing before you go. I need your help. Can you please leave a review for this book? Your feedback will help me greatly. Thank you.

ACKNOWLEDGMENTS

To my husband Dom, I'd like to thank you for watching all the Netflix movies alone while I was upstairs writing. You never complained and understood that I was *driven* to write. You took care of all the basic needs of the house, kept me fed, and made sure I stayed healthy and calm. I am the luckiest woman because you love me. Sweetie, you're the greatest!

To Nick, my son and greatest teacher, you taught me how extraordinarily strong, resilient, and compassionate a soul can be. I believe in miracles because of you. Thank you for being willing to do whatever I asked you to try. We are still a hell of a team!

Diana Henderson, my editor who took on a task greater than you realized and kept my voice in the process. You are a creative genius, and I am grateful that our paths crossed once again in this life!

John C. McGinley, what can I say to a man I admire greatly for the advocacy on behalf of people with Down syndrome. You have opened doors and moved mountains. You read my manuscript before it was edited and wrote an endorsement that still wows me. Thank you for not only doing this but for being a great guy and terrific actor!

To Kevin Goetz, Kathy Manabat and Nancy McCarty Iannios, thank you for connecting me with John C. McGinley. Without all of your involvement my happy dance would not have happened.

Abe Urquilla, you are a brilliant graphic designer who is willing to do just about anything for this technically-challenged mama. I am so grateful for your patience and expertise.

To William McDuffie, thank goodness you have the most incredible patience. You have created such a magnificent website for me and I appreciate it.

Sharon Kizziah-Homes, from publishing service providing company www.paperback-press.com, your expert guidance and listening skills helped create the book of my dreams. thank you for being a true professional when consulting with your clients, formatting and more.

Cathy Philippou, my dearest longtime friend from high school, thank you for reading the first draft of the manuscript and editing where you saw fit. I knew I could ask you without hesitation because of your steadfast encouragement and support. You are one of my greatest cheerleaders and I love you.

To Deb Muzik, you are my sage who is wiser, funnier, and prettier than Obi-Wan Kenobi. Thank you for helping me in all the ways that you do. May we continue to fly around the universe together forever.

To Diana Needham, a book marketing expert who generously gives her knowledge to inspiring writers, thank you for your wisdom.

To the beta readers who took precious time from their day and families to read and provide direct and honest feedback. Debra Branca, Phyllis Robinson, Mira Szyper, Daniel Szyper, Andrea Philippou, Jennifer Arminio, Edie Weinstein, and Michael Taubenslag, my gratitude is endless.

To my friends, you know who you are, thank you for understanding why I didn't reach out to call as often as I should have. You knew my priority was writing and getting the message out. Your love and support were appreciated.

To my unseen helpers in the spirit world, deceased loved ones, and, of course, God, I am grateful for your continual guidance and grace. I know I do not always get what I want, but I know I get what I need.

Always in your service,
Deb

RESOURCES

Special Needs Directories, Tools, Technique, Practitioners and Recommended Reading

DIRECTORIES

Insource – Special Education Parent Support
http://www.insource.org

Federation for Children with Special Needs:
https://www.fcsn.org

Special Needs Resource Directory by eparent.com
https://www.eparent.com

Special Education Guide – Support and Resources for Parents and Teachers
https://www.specialeducationguide.com

Special Needs Advocates Directory
https://www.specialneeds.com

Military Education Directory for Children with Special Needs
https://www.parentcenterhub.org

U.S. Government Special Needs Resource Directory
https://www.youth.gov

NJ Department of Human Services: NJ
Resources 2019-2020
https://www.state.nj.us/humanservices/dds/h
ome/
(Request the 146-page directory that lists
everything you could possibly need with
contact information.)

Parent to Parent USA
https://www.p2pusa.org

National Youth Leadership Network
https://www.nyln.org

National Collaborative on Workforce and
Disability for Youth
http://www.ncwd-youth.info

The M.O.R.G.A.N. Project
http://www.themorganproject.org

Partners in Policymaking – Family Support
Research and Training
http://www.partnersinpolicymaking.com

People First
https://www.peoplefirst.org

NAMI – National Alliance on Mental Illness
https://www.nami.org

ORGANIZATIONS OF TOOLS AND TECHNIQUES

American Society of Group Psychotherapy and Psychodrama
https://asgpp.org

Angel and Oracle Cards
https://hayhouse.com

National Anger Management Association
http://namass.org

Breathwork Alliance
https://breathworkalliance.com

Caregiving Resources
https://caregivingclub.com

Clinical Hypnosis: National Guild of Hypnotists
https://ngh.net

Colored Light Therapy
https://spectrahue.com

Cranial Electrotherapy Stimulation Devices
https://alpha-stim.com
https://cesultra.com

Creative Arts Therapies: National Coalition of Creative Arts Therapies Associations
https://nccata.org

Flower Remedies:
Flower Essence Society:
http://flowersociety.org
Green Hope Farm Flower Essences:
https://www.greenhopeessences.com

Mankind Project
https://mankindproject.org

Music and Sound Therapy
https://blog.mindvalley.com
Search "Everything You Need to Know About
Sound Healing."

Natal Astrological Websites (free charts)
https://cafeastrology.com
https://alabe.com
https://astro-charts.com
https://grupovenus.com

Neurofeedback
https://isnr.org

Reiki
https://reiki.org
https://iarpreiki.org

Spiritual Hypnosis
https://hypnosisfederation.com
https://nath.world

Vision Therapy
http://visiontherapy.org

PRACTITIONERS

Akashic Records Soul Coaching: Lori Chrepta
https://soul-springs.com

Astrologers:
Tara Sutphen
https://tarainsight.com

Phillip Melvin Chalk
(313) 942-6697

Psychic/Mediums:
Debra Taubenslag
https://debrataubenslag.com

Jack Keller
http://intuitivejack.com

Joyce Keller
https://joycekeller.com

Tara Sutphen
https://tarainsight.com

Thomas John
https://mediumthomas.com

Reiki:
Erin Acevedo
https://facebook.com/erinacevedopsychic

Heidi Scanlon
https://njschoolofreiki.com

Spiritual Hypnosis and Intuitive Guidance:
Debra Taubenslag
https://debrataubenslag.com

Tara Sutphen
https://tarainsight.com

RECOMMENDED READING

On Healing:

Dispenza, Joe (2014). *You are the Placebo: Making Your Mind Matter*. Carlsbad: Hay House.

Doidge, Norman (2015). *The Brain's Way of Healing*. New York: Viking.

Eden, Donna (1998). *Energy Medicine*. New York: Tarcher/Putnam.

Hay, Louise (1984). *You Can Heal Your Life*. Carlsbad: Hay House.

Motz, Julie (1998). *Hands of Life*. New York: Bantam.

Myss, Caroline (1996). *Anatomy of the Spirit.* New York: MJF Books.

Orloff, Judith (2005). *Positive Energy.* New York: Three Rivers Press.

Whiteley Hawkes, Joyce (2006). *Cell-Level Healing.* New York: Atria.

Worrall, Ambrose and Olga (1965). *The Gift of Healing.* Columbus: Ariel Press.

On Spiritual Awakening, Hypnosis and Psychic Mediumship:

Keller, Joyce (2003). *Seven Steps to Heaven.* New York: Fireside.

Smith, Philip (2008). *Walking Through Walls.* New York: Atria.

Stockwell-Nicholas, Shelley. *Hypnosis: Smile on Your Face, Money in Your Pocket,* Creativity Unlimited Press, to order: ihf@cox.net, subject: Hypnosis education

Stockwell-Nicholas, Shelley. *Hypno-Mindfulness Made Easy,* Creativity Unlimited Press, to order: ihf@cox.net, subject: Hypnosis education

Stockwell-Nicholas, Shelley. *Mindfulness for Yourself and Others*, Creativity Unlimited Press, to order: ihf@cox.net, subject: Hypnosis education

Sutphen, Dick and Tara (2005). *Soul Agreements*. Charlottesville: Hampton Roads.

Taubenslag, Debra (2000). *Not Crazy Just Enlightened*. Lakeville: Galde Press.

On Social Skills, Temperament Character Intelligence, and Parenting:

Chlan, Kathy (2017). *Maternally Challenged: How My Special Needs Son Taught Me to Sack Up and Laugh*. Kindle.

Gigante, Sophia Rose. *Stress Resilience growth* Delaware: SRG

Keirsey, David (1998). *Please Understand Me II*. Del Mar: Prometheus Nemesis.

Laugeson, Elizabeth (2017). *PEERS for Young Adults*. New York: Routledge.

Snelling, Sherri (2013). *A Cast of Caregivers: Celebrity Stories to Help You Prepare to Care*. Bloomington: Balboa Press.

Made in the USA
Middletown, DE
06 February 2021